100 QUESTIONS TO UNLEASH YOUR INNER POTENTIAL:

A GUIDE TO PERSONAL GROWTH AND TRANSFORMATION

Dr. Sophia Khousadian

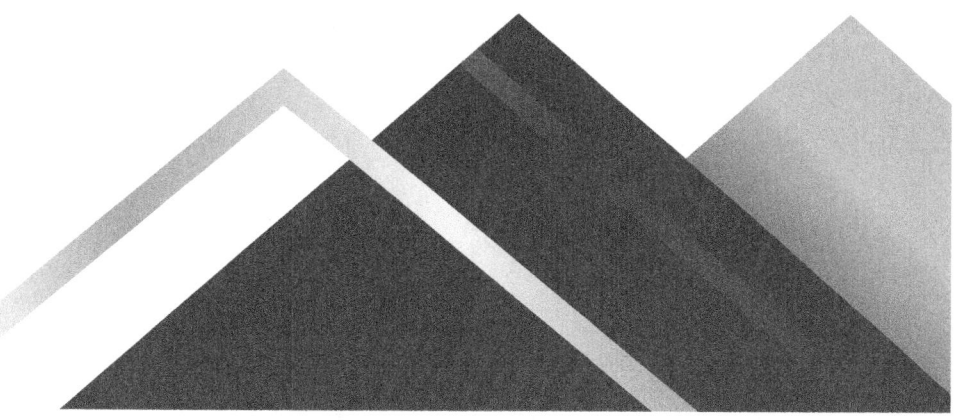

100 Questions to Unleash Your Inner Potential:
A Guide to Personal Growth and Transformation

Written by:

Dr. Sophia Khousadian

Copyright © 2023 by Dr. Sophia Khousadian
All rights reserved. This book or parts thereof may not be reproduced in any form, stored in any retrieval system, or transmitted in any form by any means — electronic, mechanical, photocopy, recording, or otherwise — without prior written permission of the publisher and author.

Preliminary Dedication

Arthur Sezgin,

Your unwavering support and guidance throughout the journey of creating this book has been nothing short of inspiring.

From the moment I embarked on this endeavor, you stood by my side as a beacon of wisdom and encouragement. Your insights, thoughtful critiques, and constructive feedback have played an instrumental role in shaping the ideas and concepts within these pages.

As I delved into the realms of self-discovery and transformation, your friendship provided a foundation. Your belief in my abilities, even during moments of doubt, has been a driving force that propelled me forward.

Your ability to understand the intricacies of personal growth and your skill for unraveling complex thoughts have illuminated my path and enriched the very essence of this book. Your genuine passion for helping others grow has left an indelible mark on these pages.

Arthur, you've been more than a friend; you've been a mentor and a pillar of strength. Your dedication to my growth mirrors the essence of this book, and I'm incredibly fortunate to have had you as a guiding light.

May the words within this book reflect the transformative power of our collaboration. As we continue to learn, evolve, and inspire, know that your influence has left an indelible imprint on every page and every reader who embarks on this journey.

With heartfelt appreciation and admiration,

Dr. Sophia Khousadian

Dedication

For Those Committed to Self-Growth and Transforming Lives

This book is dedicated to the brave souls who embark on a lifelong journey of self-growth, seeking to improve, reflect, and better their lives. It is for those who choose not to settle for mediocrity but strive for greatness in every aspect of their being. This book is a tribute to your unwavering commitment to personal development and its transformative power.

To all seekers of wisdom, self-awareness, and fulfillment, this is for you. You are the ones who recognize that true success lies in the continuous pursuit of growth, both internally and externally. You understand that becoming the best version of yourself is not easy, but you embrace the challenges with open arms.

Your dedication to self-growth is an inspiration to others. You lead by example, showing the world that change is possible and that personal transformation knows no limits. Through your relentless efforts, you ignite a spark in others, encouraging them to embark on their journey of self-discovery.

You understand the power of reflection, the art of introspection. You courageously confront your flaws, acknowledge your weaknesses, and embrace your strengths. You seek to understand the intricate depths of your being and use that knowledge to navigate through life's twists and turns.

You are not content with mere surface-level changes in your pursuit of self-improvement. Instead, you delve deeper, exploring the realms of emotional intelligence, resilience, and empathy. In addition, you strive to create meaningful connections, nurturing relationships that bring out the best in others and yourself.

Your commitment to self-growth extends beyond personal boundaries. You recognize the impact you can have on the world around you. You dedicate yourself to making a positive difference, leaving a legacy of kindness, compassion, and empowerment.

You face setbacks, obstacles, and moments of doubt throughout your journey. However, you always keep sight of your purpose. You pick yourself up, learn from your failures, and continue moving forward with unwavering determination. Your resilience is a testament to the strength of your character.

To all the souls seeking self-growth and a better life, know that you are not alone. You are part of a vibrant community of individuals united by a common goal. Reach out, support one another, and share your experiences. Together, we can create a world of self-awareness, growth, and positive change.

This is for you, the relentless pursuers of self-growth. Your journey is noble, your efforts are commendable, and your impact is immeasurable. May you continue to flourish, evolve, and inspire others.

Roadmap to Success: Nurturing Self-Growth

Success is a journey that encompasses personal growth, fulfillment, and achieving one's goals. Developing a roadmap that guides us through the process is essential to embark on this transformative path. Here is a roadmap to success, focusing specifically on self-growth:

1. **Define Your Vision:** Begin by clarifying your vision for personal success. What does success mean to you? What are your long-term goals and aspirations? Next, define your vision and set specific, measurable, achievable, relevant, and time-bound (SMART) goals that align with your vision.

2. **Cultivate Self-Awareness:** Self-awareness is the cornerstone of self-growth. Reflect on your strengths, weaknesses, values, and beliefs. Recognize your passions and interests. Identify areas where you can improve and embrace a growth mindset. Regularly engage in self-reflection and seek feedback from trusted mentors or peers.

3. **Continuous Learning:** Commit to lifelong learning. Expand your knowledge and skills through formal education, reading, attending workshops or seminars, and engaging in online courses. Embrace new challenges and explore different perspectives. Stay curious and open-minded, and be willing to step out of your comfort zone.

4. **Set Actionable Plans:** Break your long-term goals into smaller, actionable steps. Create a plan with specific milestones and deadlines. Prioritize tasks and focus on one step at a time. Celebrate small victories along the way to stay motivated and maintain momentum.

5. **Embrace Failure and Resilience:** Understand that failure is a natural part of the learning process. Embrace failure as an opportunity for growth and learning. Develop resilience by bouncing back from setbacks, learning from mistakes, and adapting your approach. Reframe challenges as stepping-stones toward success.

6. **Nurture Healthy Habits:** Cultivate habits that support your personal growth — practice self-care by prioritizing physical and mental well-being. Establish a routine that includes regular exercise, healthy eating, quality sleep, and mindfulness practices. Manage your time effectively and eliminate distractions. Surround yourself with positive influences and supportive relationships.

7. **Seek Guidance and Mentorship:** Seek guidance from mentors or role models who have achieved success in areas you aspire to grow. Learn from their experiences, seek their advice, and leverage their wisdom. Build a network of like-minded individuals who can provide support, encouragement, and accountability.

8. **Practice Self-Reflection and Gratitude:** Regularly set aside time for self-reflection. Assess your progress, reassess your goals, and make necessary adjustments. Express gratitude for the achievements, experiences, and support you receive along your journey. Cultivating gratitude enhances positivity and keeps you grounded.

9. **Give Back:** Success is not solely about personal growth but also about positively impacting others and the community. Find ways to give back, volunteer, and contribute to causes that resonate with you. Helping others fosters empathy, gratitude, and a sense of fulfillment.

10. **Celebrate Milestones:** Acknowledge and celebrate your accomplishments, both big and small. Reward yourself for reaching milestones and achieving goals. Celebrations create a positive mindset, reinforce progress, and provide motivation to continue striving for success.

Remember, the road to success is unique for everyone. So, stay committed, be adaptable, and enjoy the journey of self-growth. With dedication, perseverance, and a clear roadmap, you can unlock your potential and achieve your desired success.

Prologue: Embarking on a Journey of Self-Discovery

In the web of existence, there lies a hidden trove of untapped potential, awaiting discovery and cultivation. Life is an intricate tapestry of experiences, emotions, and aspirations, and within this tapestry resides the key to unlocking your inner potential. Welcome to "*100 Questions to Unleash Your Inner Potential: A Guide to Personal Growth and Transformation*," a journey that beckons you to traverse the landscapes of your mind, heart, and soul, and to uncover the depths of your true self.

Terms to Illuminate Your Path

Personal Growth: The intentional and continuous process of self-improvement, encompassing various aspects of your life, including emotional, intellectual, and spiritual dimensions.

Transformation: The profound shift that occurs within an individual when they embrace change, evolve, and expand their capacities beyond their current state.

Self-awareness: The foundation of personal growth, involving a deep understanding of one's thoughts, emotions, behaviors, strengths, weaknesses, and values.

Mindset: The collection of beliefs and attitudes that shape your perception of the world, influencing how you respond to challenges, setbacks, and opportunities.

Resilience: The ability to bounce back from adversity, using setbacks as stepping-stones toward growth and greater strength.

Empathy: The capacity to understand and share the feelings and perspectives of others, fostering meaningful connections and relationships.

Purpose: The driving force that gives meaning and direction to your life, helping you channel your energy toward pursuits that align with your values and aspirations.

Habits: The behaviors and routines that shape your daily life, contributing significantly to your long-term success and personal development.

Mindfulness: The practice of being fully present in the moment, cultivating awareness and attentiveness to your thoughts, feelings, and surroundings.

Meditation: A practice of calming the mind and connecting with your inner self, often involving focused breathing and self-reflection.

Self-care: The practice of nurturing your physical, emotional, and mental well-being, ensuring you have the vitality and capacity to thrive.

Gratitude: The practice of acknowledging and appreciating the positive aspects of your life, which enhances your overall sense of fulfillment.

Vulnerability: The courage to open yourself up to others and reveal your authentic self, creating space for genuine connections and personal growth.

Limiting Beliefs: Negative and restrictive thoughts that hinder your progress, often rooted in past experiences or misconceptions about your abilities.

Embarking on the Journey

As you delve into the pages of this guide, you will encounter a collection of thought-provoking questions meticulously designed to spark introspection, foster self-awareness, and guide you toward actionable steps for growth. Each question is a lantern illuminating a different facet of your inner world, encouraging you to explore uncharted territories and reevaluate preconceived notions.

This journey is not about reaching a destination; it is about embracing the ongoing process of transformation. The power lies within you to transcend limitations, expand your horizons, practice mindfulness, and uncover the limitless potential that resides within your being.

Are you ready to embark on this voyage of self-discovery? Are you prepared to challenge assumptions, break free from constraints, meditate on your thoughts, and embark on a path that leads to personal growth and transformation? The adventure begins with the turn of the page, as you take the first mindful step toward unleashing your inner potential.

There is one rule and one rule only before you proceed:

BE HONEST WITH YOURSELF.

Question #1

Are you where you want to be in life?

Let's be honest; you picked this book up for a reason. If you felt you were where you wanted to be, you wouldn't be reading this now. If you were living the life you imagined for yourself, you probably wouldn't be reflecting on these questions.

This question forces you to confront your current circumstances and assess whether they align with the vision you have for yourself. While there may be aspects of your life that have unfolded according to plan, there are undoubtedly areas where you still have work to do. This question serves as a reminder of the importance of periodically evaluating your progress and reassessing your goals. It also prompts you to consider whether you are actively taking steps toward achieving the desired life or if complacency has taken hold. Regardless of your current position, this question should motivate you to take ownership of your choices, make necessary adjustments, and continue striving toward a future that resonates with your passions, values, and aspirations.

Question #2

What drives you more? Fear or Failure?

We fear failure more than success because we are conditioned to think failure is a "bad thing." Our society tells us that if we fail, we lack significance in some area. Research has found that the fear of failure causes people to experience anxiety and helplessness and reduces resilience. Unfortunately, this then causes self-sabotage and a lack of achievement of goals. If kept in perspective, fear of failure, however it is understood, can be a catalyst to success.

This question brings to light the complexity of human motivation. While fear can be a powerful force, pushing you to act and avoid potential pitfalls, you find that the prospect of failure carries a more necessary driving power within you. Loss, often accompanied by valuable lessons and personal growth, incentivizes improvement and resilience. It pushes you to confront your limitations, learn from mistakes, and strive for continuous progress. Embracing failure as a natural part of the journey, rather than succumbing to fear, allows you to approach challenges with curiosity, perseverance, and determination to overcome obstacles.

However, it is essential to note that fear can still play a role in shaping your actions. Fear can serve as a warning sign, urging caution and prompting you to assess risks. Therefore, it is crucial to strike a balance, acknowledging and respecting legitimate fears without allowing them to paralyze you. By embracing failure as an incentive for growth and using fear as a guide rather than a deterrent, you should feel empowered to pursue your goals with courage and determination, embracing the challenges that come your way.

Fear and failure are powerful motivators, but their impact on individuals can vary depending on their mindset and personal experiences. Here's an example: Imagine two entrepreneurs, Alex and Sarah, who dream of starting their businesses. Alex is driven by fear, while Sarah is motivated by a fear of failure.

Alex's fear stems from a deep-seated fear of the unknown. He worries about the risks involved in starting a business, the possibility of financial instability, and the fear of stepping outside their comfort zone. Despite his fear, Alex channels it as a source of motivation. He meticulously plans each step, does extensive market research, and seeks advice from experienced mentors. Their fear of failure pushes them to be proactive, take calculated risks, and continuously educate themselves to diminish potential threats.

On the other hand, Sarah's driving force is the fear of failure. Sarah strongly dislikes the thought of failing in her entrepreneurial journey. This fear propels Sarah to work tirelessly, never settling for mediocrity. Instead, Sarah embraces failures as valuable learning experiences and adjusts their strategies accordingly. She meticulously analyzes her mistakes, seeks feedback from customers and mentors, and continuously iterates her business model. The fear of failure drives Sarah to persist, adapt, and improve, making failure a stepping-stone to success.

Both fear and failure can be powerful motivators, but how they drive individuals can differ. For example, while fear might cause some individuals to avoid risks altogether, the fear of failure can push others to embrace challenges and grow from setbacks. Ultimately, it's a matter of personal mindset and channeling these emotions to achieve their goals.

Question #3

What scares you about change? About your future?

Metathesiophobia, a phobia that prevents people from changing their circumstances because they are so terrified of the unknown, is the fear of change. It occasionally goes hand in hand with tropophobia, the fear of movement. People are predisposed to fear change for a variety of reasons. However, a person's fear of change could be magnified if the shift is uncontrollable. Some common forms of coping with the fear of the unknown are journaling, meditating, creating a vision board, discussing with family and friends, setting micro and macro goals, and avoiding avoidance.

One common aspect that scares us about change and the future is the fear of the unknown. Uncertainty can trigger anxiety and apprehension as we contemplate what lies ahead.

You may find yourself grappling with a mix of apprehension and uncertainty. Change, with its inherent unpredictability, triggers fear in one's heart. The fear of the unknown, of stepping into unfamiliar territory, can be scary. The fear of leaving behind the comfort and security of what is familiar disrupts your life's established routines and patterns. You may need to reflect on whether you possess the necessary skills and adaptability to navigate the shifting landscapes that change brings. The fear of failure and the potential setbacks that may accompany change cast a shadow of doubt over one's aspirations, making you question your ability to meet the challenges.

When contemplating your future, you are confronted by a similar fear. The future holds a vast expanse of possibilities, and while this can be exciting, it also presents an overwhelming prospect. You fear making the wrong choices or taking paths that may lead to unfulfillment or regret. The fear of not living up to your expectations or the expectations of others weighs heavily on your mind. Uncertainty about your career, relationships, and personal growth stirs a deep-rooted uneasiness within you. However, amidst the fear, you recognize that the future holds the potential for growth, new experiences, and self-discovery. Attempt to strike a delicate balance between acknowledging your fears and embracing the possibilities ahead, reminding yourself that courage and resilience will guide you as you navigate the uncharted terrain of your future.

Question #4

What has made you happy in the past, and what can you do to feel that way again?

The good news is that you have control over your level of happiness, that is, if you've been searching for it. Through your decisions, ideas, and deeds, you are fully capable of finding your joy. You can make yourself happier, but turning that switch is more complex. First, decide to express gratitude regularly. Choose at least one action that will enhance your life each day. When you catch yourself having an unappreciative thought, try changing it to an appreciative one. When you get up in the morning and just before you go to bed at night, consider your blessings. Only put off experiencing joy once your life is less hectic or demanding. Try to find opportunities to enjoy the little things in life. Instead of wallowing in the past or fretting about the future, concentrate on the good in the here and now.

Reflecting on what has made you happy in the past, you recall moments filled with genuine joy and contentment. Life's simple pleasures have consistently brought you happiness - spending quality time with loved ones, engaging in hobbies and passions and achieving personal milestones. The laughter and shared experiences with family and friends, the fulfillment derived from creative pursuits, and the satisfaction of personal growth and accomplishment have all contributed to your happiness. To feel that way again, you can prioritize nurturing your relationships, fostering deeper connections, and creating opportunities for shared experiences. In addition, you can carve out time for your hobbies, whether playing a musical instrument, painting, or pursuing other forms of creative expression. Setting meaningful goals and working towards them can reignite your sense of purpose and accomplishment that you have experienced in the past. Additionally, engaging in acts of kindness and giving back to the community can bring a profound sense of fulfillment and joy.

As you reflect on the question, you acknowledge that your happiness lies in actively seeking out experiences and moments that bring you joy. You understand that it is essential to prioritize physical and emotional self-care to cultivate a positive mindset. Mindfulness and gratitude can help you appreciate the present moment and find happiness in the little things. Finally, you recognize that seeking happiness is a continuous process that requires self-reflection, embracing new experiences, and embracing a growth mindset. You can create a life filled with happiness and fulfillment by remaining open to possibilities, pursuing your passions, and nurturing your relationships.

Question #5

Are you holding on to something damaging to your growth?

       The act of holding on to something is as common as breathing. We tend to hold on tight to the people we cherish and those who are significant in our lives. We also tend to keep our most priceless belongings. You may have negative mental habits you have practiced over time, and unrealistic expectations and hopes were established. Negative emotions and bad habits cause us unnecessary suffering. This excessive attachment is the origin of suffering, according to Buddhist philosophy. The Dalai Lama says most of our problems are due to our passionate desire and passion for things that we misinterpret as enduring entities. Therefore, understanding why we hold on and learning to let go of those attachments is essential to achieving mental balance and happiness—from a psychological perspective, holding on means becoming excessively and obsessively attached to something or someone, which causes us to lose perspective and objectivity entirely.

       That attachment ultimately results in a rigid stance and a constrained attitude that pushes us toward unhelpful behaviors. To learn to let go is to learn to live. That is the tragedy and irony that results from our never-ending attempt to cling on; It is futile and makes us feel the anguish we are attempting to avoid. When we realize it, we can let go of our attachment. We give the environment we live in the freedom to fulfill us without having the ability to destroy us when we stop attempting to possess and control it. Therefore, letting go allows for happiness and fulfillment.

As we explore our innermost thoughts, some elements in our lives may have deterred our progress. It might be a toxic relationship that drained your energy and self-worth or a deep-rooted fear that held you back from taking risks and pursuing your dreams. Acknowledge that holding on to these damaging elements prevents you from reaching your full potential and stifles your personal growth. With newfound clarity, you can release these dangerous attachments, let go of what no longer serves you, and embrace a path of healing and self-discovery.

Looking ahead, you may understand that releasing damaging influences and beliefs is not an easy journey. It requires courage, self-reflection, and the willingness to confront uncomfortable truths. You will recognize that personal growth requires shedding old patterns, leaving behind self-limiting beliefs, and stepping out of your comfort zone. You will embrace the idea that growth comes from embracing change, being open to new perspectives, and making choices that align with your authentic self. You will commit to promoting a mindset of self-empowerment, resilience, and self-compassion, knowing that by relinquishing what hinders your growth, you will create space for new opportunities and the blossoming of your true potential.

Question #6

If today was your last day, how would you want to spend it?

      Each of you will respond to this very differently. Some of you might not change a thing, some might spend time with family, and others will want to travel the world. Every moment becomes imbued with a profound sense of significance, as we reflect on the journey we have traversed, the memories we have woven, and the connections we have forged.

      Contemplating how you would spend your last day if today was your final breath, you embark on a soul-searching journey. You will realize that in the face of mortality, the trivial worries and material pursuits that once consumed your thoughts seem insignificant. Instead, you yearn for a day filled with meaningful connections and experiences. You will want to surround yourself with loved ones, express gratitude, and cherish the precious moments together. You will prioritize quality time, engaging in deep conversations and laughter, and creating lasting memories that transcend your physical presence.

In addition to loved ones, you may also seek solace and connection with nature. You may need to immerse yourself in the beauty of the natural world, feel the gentle caress of the wind, witness the vibrant colors of a breathtaking sunset, and bask in the serenity of a starlit night. You may crave a sense of awe and wonder, reminding yourself of the vastness of the universe and the interconnectedness of all life. Ultimately, you will understand that your last day will be a testament to the profound value of love, connection, and the awe-inspiring beauty of the world around you.

This question serves as a sympathetic reminder of life's impermanence and the importance of seizing the present moment. It prompts us to reflect on our priorities, values, and relationships, compelling us to strip away the trivial and focus on what truly matters. It's a question that urges us to break free from the routine and mundane, inviting us to savor life's simple pleasures, connect with loved ones, and leave a legacy of love and positivity. Ultimately, it underscores the profound truth that time is our most precious resource, and how we choose to spend it can define the essence of our existence.

Question #7

What are the three most valuable things in your life?

    The feeling that one's life is coherent and "makes sense," the possession of clear and gratifying long-term objectives, and the conviction that one's life matters in the grand scheme of things are all characteristics that many academics agree often come down to when defining a subjectively meaningful existence. These three concepts are referred to by psychologists as coherence, purpose, and existential mattering. However, there's also something else to consider. We occasionally have brief but exquisite moments in life. When people are willing to appreciate them, these encounters may improve how they view their lives. This component is what we term experience as appreciation.

    This phenomenon demonstrates a sense of being deeply connected to events as they happen and the capacity to derive value from that connection. It stands for the recognition and adoration of the inherent beauty of life. Life can feel more significant when we appreciate the little things. Applying such knowledge, however, might be challenging. The day is filled with objectives thanks to our contemporary, project-oriented lifestyles that move quickly. We constantly seek to increase productivity at work or in our free time. It is far too simple to overlook what is happening now when one is so intently focused on possible results. However, life takes place right now. We should take it easy, let life surprise us, and appreciate the importance of the little things in life.

Amidst the complexities of life, three treasures hold the utmost importance for you. First, you will realize that the three most valuable things in your life are the presence of loved ones, personal well-being, and the pursuit of knowledge and personal growth. These pillars provide a foundation for happiness, fulfillment, and a life of intention and purpose.

The bond you share with family and friends, built on love, trust, and support, brings you immeasurable joy and a sense of belonging. You cherish the moments of laughter, shared experiences, and the comfort of knowing you were never alone on life's journey.

An invaluable aspect of your life is your well-being. You will recognize the significance of physical, mental, and emotional health. Nurturing your body, mind, and spirit is essential for a fulfilling and meaningful existence. You will understand the importance of self-care, setting boundaries, and engaging in activities that bring joy, peace, and a sense of purpose. Prioritizing your well-being enables you to show up as your best self and positively impact those around you.

The most valuable aspect is the pursuit of knowledge and personal growth. Learning, expanding your horizons, and continuously evolving as an individual is the key to a fulfilling life. You may have sought opportunities for self-improvement through education, exploring new interests, or embracing challenges. You will learn to treasure the moments of self-reflection, self-discovery, and the ever-present desire to become a better version of yourself.

Question #8

What have you given up, lost, or quit that has made you stronger?

  Everybody has challenging times in life. It can give us the strength we need to get through anything. Going through difficult times is advantageous. You become more resilient, robust, and prosperous as a result. According to psychologists, traumatic experiences might make you more resilient. People who have experienced post-traumatic growth, according to research, report improvements in their interpersonal connections, a greater appreciation for life, and new opportunities. The act of overcoming difficulty has a benefit. You'll grow more robust and successful if you endure difficult situations. You frequently meet people who have experienced hardship firsthand and are the wisest and most well-rounded. They have incredible tales to tell and have overcome obstacles. Let's explore how adversity can make you more resilient and prosperous. The following is a list of how difficult times make you stronger and more successful:

1. *You realize what matters to you*
2. *You realize it's part of the process*
3. *The taste of success is sweeter*
4. *You develop more empathy*
5. *You think more positively*

In the journey of life, there will be numerous instances where you have given up, lost, or quit certain things that have ultimately contributed to your growth and strength. One notable example is the decision to let go of toxic relationships that were draining your emotional well-being. Although it is difficult to release these connections, doing so allows you to reclaim your sense of self-worth, establish healthier boundaries, and prioritize your own happiness. Additionally, choosing to quit habits that hinder your personal development, such as negative self-talk and self-doubt. By relinquishing these destructive patterns, you will foster a more positive mindset and cultivate a stronger belief in your abilities. While the process of giving up, losing, or quitting can be challenging, it will undoubtedly forge resilience that continues to propel you forward on your journey of self-discovery and growth.

In reflection, you will understand that the things you have given up, lost, or quit have paved the way for personal growth and inner strength. The tendency for attachment and the need for external validation allowed you to embrace authenticity, resilience, and self-determination. These experiences have shaped you into the person you are today.

Question #9

Is there someone in your life that makes you want to be better?

       It may seem obvious that someone should be in your life when a relationship with them makes you a better person. They are souls that enter our narrative to forge wonderful and enlightening connections between two lives, even with unlike backgrounds, life experiences, and worldviews. They are those who offer us support, safety, and solace. People who lighten our load and make life more enjoyable, people who feel at home in their hug. Those with inner beauty and warmth who are beautiful. People help us realize that we are genuinely wealthy once we possess something with feelings that money cannot buy. People who teach us that this world is a good place with many learning opportunities are those with whom we share an unbreakable harmony. Due to this, some turn our house into a home and then into our heaven. When they enter your life, you know they belong there because you two improve one another as humans. Together, you create a wonderful atmosphere of kindness that illuminates emotional development. People who make you feel at home, those made of stainless steel, are the ones who hold you so tightly that all your pieces go back into place and who cause all your worries and woes to fade away. Those who instill in you a sense of the positive aspects of life and demonstrate how wonderful the world is.

Whether someone in your life inspired you to become a better person, you may find yourself reflecting on a particular individual who has profoundly impacted your journey. This person, whether a friend, family member, or mentor, possesses qualities and values that ignite a desire for self-improvement within you. Their presence alone reminds you of the transformative power of kindness, empathy, and compassion.

Observing the actions and behavior of this influential figure, you may feel deep admiration and respect. Witnessing their unwavering integrity, resilience in the face of challenges, and dedication to making a positive difference in the world fuels your aspirations. This person's ability to uplift others, coupled with their genuine care and support, inspires you to strive for personal growth, cultivate your virtues, and live in alignment with your values.

Acknowledge the immense impact this person has on your life. Their presence is a guiding light and encourages you to be kinder, compassionate, and resilient. Recognize the transformative power of having someone who believes in you and inspires you to embrace your full potential and make a meaningful difference in the world. With gratitude in your heart, you honor this person's influence by continuing to strive towards becoming the best version of yourself and positively impacting the lives of others.

Question #10

When was the last time you did something for the first time?

      There are so many firsts in life. As you reflect upon your life's firsts, you will have some positive and negative memories. You should always seek out new experiences and learn new things. It makes each day full of hope and enthusiasm. Your life's purpose will become apparent as you live out your true purpose and experience all the new adventures it brings. The brain is kept active by engaging in new activities. According to neuroscientists, the brain is programmed to appreciate originality and challenges. As you enter problem-solving mode, new experiences and difficulties trigger the brain to create dopamine. Dopamine is crucial for keeping the brain in good shape, and it has been shown that severe depression is related to decreased dopamine transmission. It regulates the flow of information to other areas of the brain and has an impact on movement, motivation, and the experience of pleasure. We notice reduced memory, cognitive abilities, and attention when dopamine is absent. Having more dopamine causes you to feel elated and "high" by acting similarly to adrenalin. Stress, inactivity, and poor diet all lower dopamine levels. What does this all imply? A happy brain is a brain that is stimulated! Adding new hobbies to your life will boost your happiness and enthusiasm, benefiting your physical and mental health.

 Contemplating the question of the last time you did something for the first time, you will find yourself reflecting on a recent experience that ignited a sense of novelty and adventure within you. These experiences remind you of the importance of embracing new experiences, stepping out of your comfort zone, and seeking opportunities to ignite your sense of exploration.

 Acknowledge that doing something for the first time injects a sense of vitality and growth into your life. It serves as motivation for personal development and expands your horizon. You will realize that engaging in novel experiences offers a fresh perspective, challenges preconceived notions, and nurtures curiosity. You may understand that the last time you did something for the first time reminds you of life's limitless possibilities and the importance of embracing each day as an opportunity for discovery and growth.

Question #11

When was the last time you pushed yourself out of your comfort zone?

    A comfort zone is a psychological state in which things feel familiar to a person; they are at ease and in control of their environment, experiencing low anxiety and stress levels. Therefore, it is reasonable to predict that venturing beyond one's comfort zone may cause anxiety and stress. So, what would motivate us to do that? Many psychologists and social scientists think that stepping outside of your comfort zone might improve levels of concentration and focus. Alasdair White, who coined the phrase "comfort zone," suggested that one must endure a certain degree of stress to function well. The following are the top 5 reasons to start moving outside your comfort zone:

1. *Your experiences — not just the ones you find comfortable — make up your "real life." Therefore, being fully immersed in your "real life" is crucial to developing a well-rounded personality.*

2. *You can access your store of untapped knowledge and resources by pushing yourself. When you're not challenged, you don't know what you know or how powerful you are.*

3. *Taking risks is a learning experience, regardless of the result. Failure is the first attempt at learning.*

4. *Relieving relative safety comes at an exceedingly expensive cost — settling for mediocrity. It's unacceptable to let your comfort determine how you live.*

5. *You may increase your comfort zone by stepping outside of it and learning how to handle change.*

The question, "When was the last time you pushed yourself out of your comfort zone?" holds immense significance in personal growth and self-reflection. By pondering this question, you are prompted to assess your willingness to embrace challenges and step beyond the familiar. In addition, it serves as a reminder that progress often requires venturing into the unknown and facing discomfort head-on. Reflecting on your response, you can better understand your ability to adapt, persevere, and discover hidden strengths within yourself.

This question encourages you to break free from complacency and routine. It guides exploring new opportunities, acquiring new skills, and broadening one's perspective. Stepping out of the comfort zone fosters personal development by expanding horizons, encouraging resilience, and boosting self-confidence. It empowers individuals to overcome self-imposed limitations and unlocks their potential for growth and achievement. Ultimately, the question is a powerful reminder that the path to personal evolution lies in pushing boundaries, embracing discomfort, and embracing the transformative power of stepping outside one's comfort zone.

Question #12

What changes can you make to ensure you are working on being the best version of yourself?

　　　　Living genuinely is the key to being your best self. You must be loyal to who you are and what you stand for to be your best self. Additionally, you must ensure that the activities you are engaged in provide you with a sense of fulfillment, purpose, and significance. Being your best self is about what you can manage, not whether life is easy or perfect. Sustainability is also important. You wouldn't want to give up your tomorrow to live as you do now. Understanding and realizing your potential is essential to being your best self. Intrinsic and extrinsic motivation are the two different forms of motivation. Motivation from within would be best defined as inherent. This is when your beliefs and values are the foundation for your intrinsic motivation. For instance, you desire to improve because you delight in challenges. Motivation from without would be best described as extrinsic. On the other hand, extrinsic motivation is brought on by outside forces like reward, acknowledgment, or escape from punishment.
　　　　For instance, you can improve yourself to impress your close friends or get a job promotion. Whichever it may be, keep sight of your

motivation to improve. Then, use it as a compass to keep on course for your objectives. The route is far, and the challenges stimulating, but the strategy is straightforward. The following nine ways steps will allow you to become the best version of yourself:

1) Visualize Your Future Self;
2) Tackle Your Goals;
3) Ensure Your Goals Match Your Purpose;
4) Offer Yourself Unconditional Love;
5) Stop the Fear of Failure;
6) Stop Procrastinating;
7) Stop People Pleasing;
8) Stop Criticizing and Judging Others;
9) Stop The Negative Self-Talk.

This question holds tremendous significance in personal development and self-improvement. It prompts you to evaluate your current state and identify areas for growth and enhancement. Reflecting on this question encourages you to take ownership of your journey and actively pursue self-improvement. By acknowledging the need for change, you can set goals, develop strategies, and make conscious choices that align with your vision of becoming the best version of yourself.

This encourages you to regularly assess your actions, habits, and beliefs and identify areas for adjustments. Self-awareness allows you to identify strengths to leverage and weaknesses to address, fostering a proactive approach to personal development. The question empowers you to embrace a growth mindset, seek learning opportunities, and make intentional choices that align with your values and aspirations. By consistently striving to be the best version of yourself, you can experience personal fulfillment, achieve your goals, and contribute positively to the world around you.

Question #13

Is there anyone/anything "toxic" you are keeping in your life that you need to let go of?

You will meet "toxic" people throughout your life. It's unavoidable, whether it's a hostile family member, a friend who doesn't value your time, or a scheming boss. While it may seem inconvenient, these people can harm your health and well-being. They can take up a lot of your time and energy. You should be able to recognize the warning signs. These include:

- *Self-indulgence or selfishness*
- *Coercion and other forms of emotional/mental abuse*
- *Difficulty of dishonesty*
- *Deception compassion*
- *Has the propensity to stir up trouble or conflict*

This question carries significant weight on personal well-being and emotional health. Reflecting on this question invites you to evaluate the relationships and influences in your life and assess their impact on your overall happiness and growth. In addition, it prompts you to identify and acknowledge the presence of toxic individuals or elements hindering your progress or causing emotional harm. Recognizing and addressing these toxic factors can create a healthier, more supportive environment that nurtures your personal and emotional well-being.

Contemplating this question also encourages you to prioritize self-care and set healthy boundaries. In addition, it prompts you to consider the impact of negative influences on your mental, emotional, and even physical health. Letting go of toxic people or situations that drain energy and foster negativity can create space for personal growth, positivity, and healthy relationships. By recognizing the need to let go of toxic elements, you empower yourself to cultivate a more fulfilling and harmonious life surrounded by individuals and circumstances that uplift and support your well-being.

Question #14

What adjectives would you use to describe yourself?

　　　　　Do you love yourself enough to speak positively to yourself? Negativity from someone else is terrible enough, but when it originates inside you, that's tough. What you say to yourself in your thoughts is called self-talk. It is the inner monologue you experience whenever you drive through traffic, speak with your boss, engage in a challenging chat with a friend, or commute to work. Believe it or not, you are the most influential person in your thoughts, and the language you choose to talk to yourself is crucial. Yes, other people can undoubtedly affect how we feel and think, but ultimately, it is up to us whether we accept their messages. Unfortunately, we decide whether to accept the negativity of others, no matter what they say or do. If you tend to do this, be aware that *you* are speaking, not the other person, when you accept and repeat those negative words. Their disapproval has now entered your internal dialogue. Your self-talk, whether positive or negative, can strengthen or break you. The following is meant to increase your level of awareness, help you determine whether you're talking to yourself positively or negatively, and show you how to change your perspective. Hence, it's more upbeat:

1) Replace the Negativity;
2) Reassure Yourself;
3) Relabel Your Talk;
4) Relate to Yourself;
5) Reinterpret Your Truth;
6) Rescue Yourself;
7) Reanalyze the Information.

Reflecting on this question prompts you to dig deeper into introspection and explore your qualities, characteristics, and values. By identifying and selecting adjectives to describe yourself, you gain a deeper understanding of your identity, strengths, and areas for growth. This process of self-reflection contributes to developing a well-rounded self-concept and aids in building self-confidence and self-acceptance.

Moreover, this question encourages you to consider how you present yourself to others and how you want to be perceived. It allows you to align your self-perception with your desired values and aspirations. Selecting adjectives that reflect your authentic self will enable you to define your brand and shape your interactions and relationships. This reflection can serve as a guide for personal growth and help you strive toward becoming the best version of yourself as you work on embodying the adjectives that genuinely resonate with your values and desired self-image.

Question #15

Are you doing enough for the people you love?

People are the center of life. We don't all need to be in many relationships, but we should be around people who understand us. To feel safe and included in the world, we all require these types of deep relationships. We need those who care about us, watch out for us, accept us, bring out the best in us, and push us to be the best versions of ourselves. We may act on their behalf. It may be the family you picked, the one you were born into, or the one that chose you after tearing down the substantial wall you built to protect yourself. These relationships make everything else feel manageable, no matter who or how big your community is.

A call or a hug from the right person can serve as a reminder that life is, in fact, worth living, regardless of whether you are having a difficult day, week, month, or year. When things are going well, having the people you love beside you makes it even more joyful. Most of us concur that our relationships are what matter most. A job loss or missed opportunity is tolerable if the people we care about are secure. When we're buried in the hardships of our daily lives, it's all too easy to lose sight of the big picture. When stressed about our bills and deadlines, it's simple to put off the tiny things that maintain healthy relationships. We are wired that way to protect ourselves. Intend to be:

1. *Present*
2. *Listen Deeply*
3. *Speak Truthfully*
4. *Accept Fully*
5. *Interpret Compassionately*
6. *Forgive Often*
7. *Appreciate Vocally*
8. *Give Freely*
9. *Remain Unbiased*
10. *Love*

Reflecting on this question prompts you to evaluate your efforts and investments in relationships with loved ones. It serves as a reminder to prioritize and actively engage in acts of love, support, and care. As a result, you can assess whether you are dedicating sufficient time, attention, and effort to foster healthy and fulfilling connections with the people who matter most in your life.

Furthermore, this question encourages you to show empathy and compassion towards your loved ones. It prompts you to consider the needs, desires, and well-being of those you hold dear. It also reminds you to check in with your loved ones, ask questions, listen attentively, and help when needed. By striving to do enough for the people you love, you deepen your bond, strengthen trust, and contribute to the happiness and fulfillment of yourself and your loved ones. Ultimately, this question is a guiding compass, inspiring you to grow and improve as partners and family members continuously.

Question #16

Do others' opinions truly impact you?

Your sense of self-worth is inversely correlated with what others think of you. You always end up compliant with other people's desires. Running around and making decisions to appease everyone and ignoring your own needs. By trying to please everyone, you end up repressing your ambitions and bending and shaping yourself to conform to what you "should" be according to others. You no longer feel like you can be authentic.

You live on other people's terms when you consider their opinions as more important than your own. On the other hand, you will regret not having lived a life that was genuinely true to who you are as you lay to rest. Those people will be long gone, along with their opinions of you. You'll then question why you granted them such control over you. When caring about other's opinions, you wouldn't have lived the life you genuinely sought, needed, or wanted to live. You are then in a position where you won't give your friends, potential lovers, and/or clients a chance to get to know you honestly and realize how amazing you are; instead, you'll give them the bare minimum of what you think they'll like.

They won't be dating the real you; they'll be dating a shell. As a result, you'll deprive yourself of genuine intimacy and success. Until you stop caring what other people say and start listening to your true desires, voice, and truth, you will not be able to truly impact and feel the impact you are making in the world. The following steps will help you let go of other's opinions mattering:

1. *Take Responsibility*
2. *Let Go of the fear of Embarrassment*
3. *Stop Comparing*
4. *Increase Self-Esteem and Self-Worth*
5. *Set Boundaries*
6. *Remind Yourself Whose Life This Is*
7. *Make The Decision*
8. *Forget About Failure*
9. *Check-In with Your People*

This shows profound importance in shaping one's self-perception and personal autonomy. Reflecting on this question prompts you to examine how external opinions influence your thoughts, actions, and overall sense of self-worth. It encourages you to develop self-awareness and discernment, recognizing that while the perspectives of others can provide valuable insights and feedback, their opinions should not define or dictate one's identity or choices. Embracing this question empowers you to develop a strong sense of self, trust your judgment, and make decisions aligned with your values and aspirations rather than being solely guided by the expectations and judgments of others.

Question #17

What are some of your passions?

       We are driven to do the things we love because of our passion. This intense desire makes your ability to produce something extraordinary possible, also serving as your fire's fuel. A sense of purpose is given to you when you are passionate about something. You get a sense of meaning from it and the conviction that your life is designed for greatness. The following list consists of areas where one's passions can become forms of motivation and niches:

1. *Education/Learning*
2. *Creativity*
3. *Personal Growth*
4. *Mindfulness*
5. *Helping and Uplifting Others*
6. *Decluttering*
7. *Health and Fitness*
8. *Career Growth*
9. *Money Management*
10. *Relationship Health*

This question encourages you to explore your genuine interests and the activities that ignite your enthusiasm and purpose. Identifying and acknowledging one's passions allows for a deeper connection to oneself, enabling you to pursue activities that bring you joy and fulfillment. Passion-driven pursuits fuel motivation, creativity, and a sense of purpose, leading to a more satisfying and meaningful life. By actively considering and pursuing your passions, you can experience a greater understanding of self-fulfillment and engage in activities that resonate deeply with your values and aspirations.

Prioritizing self-care and nourishing your well-being are vital. Engaging in activities that you are passionate about can serve as a form of self-expression, stress relief, and personal rejuvenation. Passionate pursuits provide an avenue for personal growth, learning, and self-improvement. They can also lead to new opportunities, connections, and a sense of belonging within communities of like-minded individuals. By embracing and pursuing your passions, you enrich your life, expand your horizons, and support a more profound sense of purpose and fulfillment. Pursuing one's passion also helps become the best version of oneself by fostering a deep sense of purpose and fulfillment. When we engage in activities that ignite our passion, we tap into a boundless well of motivation and enthusiasm that propels us forward even in the face of obstacles. Passion provides the fuel to persevere through challenges and the resilience to learn from failures. As we immerse ourselves in our passions, we gain valuable skills and knowledge, constantly pushing the boundaries of our abilities. This continuous growth and learning process not only enhances our expertise in the chosen field but also expands our horizons, opening up new opportunities for personal and professional development. Moreover, following our passions encourages authenticity, as it aligns our actions with our true selves, instilling a profound sense of contentment and authenticity in our lives. Embracing our passions not only enriches our own lives but also allows us to inspire others to follow their dreams and create a positive impact in the world.

Question #18

Are you doing enough for yourself?

Reflecting on whether you are doing enough for yourself is a crucial exercise in self-awareness and self-care. It prompts you to assess if your current actions, decisions, and priorities align with your personal well-being and long-term goals. It's easy to get caught up in the demands of daily life, work, and responsibilities, neglecting your own needs in the process. By asking yourself this question, you open the door to explore areas where you may need to make adjustments or invest more time and energy in self-nurturing activities. Remember that self-care isn't selfish; it's a vital aspect of maintaining a healthy and balanced life. Taking time to pause, reflect, and recalibrate ensures that you can continue to give your best to others while also fostering a stronger and more resilient relationship with yourself.

Thus, the question is: At what point does productivity turn toxic? Although it may manifest differently for each of us, feeling exhausted or having poor self-worth (i.e., trying to please others or never feeling like we are good enough, and not living our truth or acting authentically) are good signs that productivity has deteriorated. It makes sense that we sometimes end up going overboard. When you are in drive, your biology is working as it should. Your brain is adapted to drive mode when you don't have enough resources and must scavenge for limited resources (food, shelter, a partner). Our brains are constantly bombarded with messages that we need to work harder, do more to keep up, or catch up thanks to modern messaging (media, social media, education system). The freedom to choose and disconnect our actions from our worth is vital. The freedom to choose and disconnect our actions from our worth is vital for fostering a healthy sense of self and promoting personal growth. Recognizing that our value as individuals is not solely determined by the outcomes of our actions empowers us to make mistakes, learn from them, and strive for improvement without fear of judgment or condemnation. By embracing this mindset, we liberate ourselves from the paralyzing grip of perfectionism and cultivate resilience, allowing us to explore new opportunities and take risks with confidence. This detachment of worth from action grants us the space to evolve, develop compassion for ourselves and others, and ultimately lead a more fulfilling and authentic life.

This question prompts you to assess the level of attention, care, and investment you dedicate to *your* needs, desires, and growth. It encourages you to prioritize self-reflection and self-compassion, recognizing that taking care of oneself is not selfish but essential for overall health and happiness. By contemplating this question, you can identify areas where you may neglect your well-being and consciously nurture yourself physically, mentally, and emotionally.

This question invites you to evaluate your work-life balance and set boundaries that prioritize your needs. In addition, it serves as a reminder that self-care is not a luxury but a fundamental aspect of a healthy and balanced life. By dedicating time to engaging in activities that bring joy, practicing self-care rituals, and pursuing personal interests, you can replenish your energy, reduce stress, and enhance your overall quality of life. Ultimately, this question empowers you to prioritize your well-being and cultivate a harmonious relationship with yourself, leading to a more fulfilled and purposeful existence.

Question #19

What's the best thing you've ever done for yourself?

Right now, you can take care of a few little things that will help you focus on your needs. Do you need to feel productive and rearrange your closet before you can feel better, or do you need to rest and heal first? Do you need a meal that makes you feel like a kid again, or do you need healthy whole grains and fresh vegetables to feel your best? Make your happiness your top priority and base your decisions on how much joy they will provide you. Once you realize how to achieve happiness is the best thing in the world, you will find peace in yourself.

This question prompts profound reflection on moments of self-care, personal growth, and life-altering decisions. Reflecting on this question invites you to revisit transformative experiences that have had a lasting positive impact on your life. It encourages a deeper understanding of the power of self-investment and the rewards that come from prioritizing personal well-being. Reflecting on this question, you can celebrate your choices that have brought personal fulfillment and happiness.

This question serves as a reminder of the importance of self-discovery and self-empowerment. It highlights the significance of taking bold steps outside of one's comfort zone, pursuing dreams and passions, and embracing opportunities for personal growth. It reinforces the value of self-belief, self-care, and courageous decision-making. Finally, it inspires individuals to continue making choices that honor their true selves and lead to fulfillment and authenticity.

Doing something for yourself is an empowering act of self-love and personal growth. It is a conscious decision to prioritize your well-being and happiness, acknowledging that you deserve time and attention just as much as anyone else in your life. Whether it's pursuing a hobby that brings you joy, taking a much-needed break to rest and recharge, embarking on a journey of self-discovery, or simply pampering yourself with some self-care, these moments are invaluable for your overall mental, emotional, and physical health. When you invest in yourself, you nourish your inner strength and resilience, allowing you to navigate life's challenges with greater confidence and grace. Remember, taking time to nurture yourself is not selfish; it's an essential ingredient in living a fulfilled and contented life.

Question #20

What are you most grateful for in your life?

    The society in which we live is predominantly filled with problems looking to be solved. We want to change so many things about who we are. Frequently, we find ourselves losing sight of the gratitude we should hold for what we already possess, both in terms of personal growth and the potential to positively impact society. It is essential to reflect on the blessings and opportunities that have shaped us as individuals and the contributions we can make to the improve the world around us. This sense of gratitude not only keeps us grounded but also fuels our desire to continuously improve ourselves and play an active role in creating positive change. By acknowledging and appreciating our current strengths and privileges, we become more conscious of the responsibility to use them for the greater good. Cultivating this gratitude and awareness can lead to a more compassionate and fulfilling journey of self-improvement, as well as a deeper commitment to making a meaningful difference in the lives of others and the broader community.

    We place so much emphasis on the bad that the good starts to fade from our hearts. The following is a list of little and big things in life we should be grateful for:

1. *Your Life*
2. *Your Situation*
3. *Your Family & Friends*

4. *Your Courage*
5. *Your Strength*
6. *Your Mind*
7. *Your Heart*
8. *Your Senses*
9. *The Things You Love*
10. *Your Belongings*
11. *Your Tears*
12. *Your Mistakes*
13. *Your Life Lessons*
14. *You Mentors*
15. *Your Happiness*
16. *Your Disappointments*
17. *Your Job*
18. *Your Enemies*
19. *Your Teachers*
20. *Your Heartbreaks*
21. *Your Laughter*
22. *Your Body*
23. *Your Pain*
24. *Nature*
25. *Your Privileges*
26. *Your Choices*

The question "What are you most grateful for in your life?" prompts deep reflection on the blessings and positive aspects that bring joy and appreciation. Reflecting on this question allows you to reflect on your gratitude and acknowledge the abundance and meaningful connections in your life. It serves as a reminder to shift focus from what may be lacking or challenging to the countless blessings, relationships, experiences, and opportunities that enrich one's existence. By meditating on this question, you can improve your mindset of gratitude, which has been shown to enhance overall well-being, foster resilience, and nurture positive relationships. It encourages you to cherish and celebrate the present moment, fostering contentment and a greater appreciation for the richness of life.

Question #21

When was the last time you made a positive change in your life?

       Most of us need help to keep up with how quickly the world in which we live is changing. Our lives are very busy with work, kids, social activities, and maintaining our homes. There needs to be more time in the day for goal-setting and fantasizing. It's challenging to navigate life with the mindset that work, eat, sleep, and repeat is all there is. The issue is that it isn't.

       Life is so much more than your everyday routine. Self-improvement can help you live a better life and reflect on the person you want to be rather than the one you are fighting to remain. Try making as many positive changes as possible when life feels terrible, and you're unsure how to achieve what you need. The magic happens when you start to change yourself and then begin to change the outside world. The world outside your front door will look like however you imagine to be if you anticipate it as difficult, stressful, and lacking adequate affection or support.

Why not concentrate on bringing about the positive changes in your life that you want to see the most rather than feeling helpless and unable to embrace self-growth? Why not publicly declare that you will not tolerate any more negativity? You won't always be able to stop problems and unpleasant events from happening, but you will always have to deal with them. However, you have power over how you respond to those difficult circumstances and can decide to be more upbeat. The best thing you can do if you feel stuck in life and can't see a way out is to start working on improving your life.

Feeling stuck in life can be a daunting and frustrating experience, leaving one with a sense of hopelessness and uncertainty. However, the most empowering step to take in such moments is to proactively work on improving your life. Embracing this mindset shifts the focus from dwelling on the challenges to actively seeking solutions and growth. It might not be easy, but taking even small steps towards positive change can create a ripple effect, leading to newfound opportunities and perspectives. Remember, every journey starts with a single step, and by choosing to work on self-improvement, you pave the way for a brighter and more fulfilling future, allowing yourself to break free from the confines of stagnation and embrace the endless possibilities life has to offer.

The most significant step you can take is to decide to lean into your fear of change. It's fun to remember that, as an adult, you are the only person who can stop you. Your life will improve if you can figure out what it is about it that makes you unhappy and then figure out how to alter it. You must consider the reasonable adjustments you want to make and then seize the opportunity with both hands if you want to put yourself first. Do what is best because you only have one chance to do this well.

By acknowledging and celebrating these moments of positive change, you are inspired to continue embracing opportunities for personal development, ultimately leading to a more fulfilling and purpose-driven life.

Question #22

What can you do to improve your self-reflection?

　　　　Simple reflection is thoughtful consideration. However, more complex introspection than that is the kind that genuinely benefits leaders. The most fruitful reflection entails consciously examining and evaluating ideas and behaviors with the aim of learning. Reflection allows the brain to stop amid chaos, organize observations and experiences, consider many interpretations, and create meaning. Learning from this meaning can then influence future actions and mindsets. This "meaning-making" for leaders is essential to their continuing development. Therefore, it is crucial to identify questions, select a reflection process that matches one's preferences, schedule time, start small, and, most importantly, do it. Finally, don't be ashamed to ask for help.
　　　　Not being ashamed to ask for help is a powerful reminder of the strength found in vulnerability. Recognizing that we all face challenges and limitations at various points in our lives, seeking assistance demonstrates courage and self-awareness. Asking for help does not diminish our worth; instead, it empowers us to grow, learn, and connect with others on a deeper level. Embracing this notion encourages a supportive and compassionate community, fostering an environment

where people can openly share their struggles and offer support without judgment. It is through seeking help that we realize we are not alone in our journey, and by reaching out, we unlock the potential for growth, healing, and ultimately, a more resilient and fulfilling life.

Improving self-reflection requires a conscious effort and a commitment to personal growth. Firstly, setting aside dedicated time for introspection is crucial. By regularly reflecting, whether daily, weekly, or monthly, you can better understand your thoughts, emotions, and actions.

Secondly, being open and honest with yourself is essential. It's important to embrace both your strengths and weaknesses without judgment. By acknowledging areas for improvement and learning from past experiences, you can cultivate self-awareness and make meaningful changes.

The idea that self-reflection doesn't necessarily require a formal process like meditation resonates deeply with me. It beautifully highlights that self-awareness can be woven into the fabric of our everyday lives, making it accessible and practical for everyone. These seemingly ordinary moments, like sitting in traffic or savoring a morning coffee, become invaluable opportunities to introspect, understand our emotions, and gain insights into our thoughts and actions. Embracing self-reflection during these simple times allows us to connect with ourselves authentically and without pressure, enabling a continuous and natural growth process. We should find comfort in knowing that self-awareness is not confined to a specific setting or activity; rather, it's an ongoing journey that enriches our lives and leads to a deeper understanding of ourselves and the world around us.

Additionally, seeking feedback from trusted individuals can provide valuable insights and perspectives that enhance self-reflection. Lastly, practicing self-compassion and kindness is vital during this process, as it allows you to accept yourself as a work in progress and encourages a growth mindset. By dedicating time, embracing honesty, seeking feedback, and practicing self-compassion, you can continually enhance your self-reflection skills and foster personal development.

Question #23

Are you challenging yourself daily?

Your daily routine, habits, and activities are the keys to your success — and any success — in life. Nothing worthwhile ever comes overnight, no matter what you aim for or how you define success. A single step always marks the beginning of a transformation. You do not necessarily need to know the appropriate second or third step. Instead, you can start by taking that first step. One of the most crucial components of self-improvement is challenging oneself. There can be neither improvement nor growth without challenge and change. We frequently express our aspirations and dreams by talking about them, but that is all that ever happens. We aren't always willing to put ourselves through a challenge, leave our comfort zone, and act. It could seem difficult to face challenge and change, to take on tasks that terrify or frighten us, but it doesn't have to be.

Reflecting on whether you are challenging yourself daily is an opportunity to assess your personal growth and strive for continuous improvement. First, you must evaluate your daily activities' difficulty and novelty level. Challenging yourself means stepping out of your comfort zone and actively seeking opportunities to learn, grow, and push your limits. It involves setting ambitious goals, embracing new experiences, and taking calculated risks. You can expand your knowledge, skills, and perspectives by constantly seeking challenges.

Self-reflection allows you to assess whether you are proactively seeking growth or becoming complacent in your daily routines. Challenging yourself daily involves a mindset shift that embraces discomfort and the unknown. It requires discipline and a willingness to explore new ideas, tackle complex tasks, and persist through obstacles. By pushing your boundaries, you can develop resiliency, creativity, and adaptability, essential personal and professional development qualities. Regularly assessing whether you are challenging yourself daily reminds you to stay proactive, embrace growth opportunities, and strive for continuous self-improvement.

Question #24

Do you confide in others or bottle up your emotions?

      It is not easy to talk about your feelings. It can seem awkward, helpless, and downright impossible. Many of us occasionally wonder if discussing our emotions is worthwhile. Humans are very emotional creatures. We go through a wide range of emotions throughout the day due to who we are and the environment we live in. What occurs then if we don't discuss our issues with others? They typically accumulate inside of us. We are not just emotional but also incredibly sociable. We flourish when we have meaningful relationships with other people and experience a deep sense of belonging. It's crucial to have someone in our lives that we can confide in and talk to. Using this venting procedure, we may let go of the emotions that so quickly bubble up inside us.

      Additionally, these venting processes enhance our feelings of acceptance and support from the people in our lives. Numerous individuals can partake in this cathartic practice, whether it involves sharing with a broader social media network or confiding in close friends, family members, a significant other, a therapist, or joining a support group.

Reflecting on whether you confide in others or bottle up your emotions brings awareness to your approach to dealing with your inner world. It is essential to recognize that emotions are a natural part of being human, and acknowledging and expressing them healthily is vital for your overall well-being. Bottling up emotions can increase stress, anxiety, and even cause or exacerbate physical health issues. By confiding in others, you can benefit from the support, empathy, and perspective they could offer.

Sharing your emotions with trusted individuals creates a space for you to be vulnerable and allows others to provide comfort, guidance, and a sense of acceptance. It fosters connection and strengthens relationships. However, it is also essential to balance and exercise discernment in choosing whom to confide in, ensuring that the individuals are trustworthy and supportive.

Additionally, seeking professional help, such as therapy or counseling, can provide a safe and confidential environment to explore and process your emotions. Overall, reflecting on your approach to confiding in others versus bottling up your feelings highlights the significance of emotional well-being and emphasizes the value of seeking support and connection in navigating life's challenges.

Question #25

What is the biggest lesson you've learned thus far?

This question will require some reflection. What may be a big lesson for you may not hold the same weight for someone else. So here is a list of life lessons that can hopefully resonate with you or allow you to reflect on where you presently stand in your life:

1. *Life is unpredictable. In a split second, your entire life can change. Be thankful for what you have and use it to your advantage rather than passively taking it for granted.*
2. *You owe nothing to your younger self but everything to your present self.*
3. *You can't think your way into a new life; you must take action to do so because action produces more clarity than the idea.*
4. *Amidst the pursuit of happiness, one might encounter moments of misery, only to eventually discover that happiness itself is the very path to follow.*

5. *If you aspire to change the trajectory of your life, embrace, and adhere to these principles: Commitment, consistency, and persistence form the three pillars of success. It is commitment that serves as the driving force to initiate your journey.*
6. *We slowly degrade over time, but we also care for ourselves and rebuild ourselves, little by little, over time. Why? Because your habits make up who you are, what you do today will determine who you are tomorrow.*
7. *You'll remain motivated if you share your progress rather than your objectives.*
8. *Cease comparing yourself to others and constructing your version of success solely on their terms. It is feasible to build a meaningful and fulfilling life, but pursuing your passions does not necessarily mean life becomes easier; instead, it fosters greater discipline and happiness.*
9. *Everything you do, whether right or wrong, stems from a set of beliefs. This suggests that self-care involves digging deep inside to uncover all the unconscious behavioral and cognitive habits potentially impeding your growth.*
10. *Aim to slow down in this age of acceleration and speed. When you live slowly, you start caring for your body, mind, and soul so they can care for you. You also become more mindful and intentional about how you live your life.*
11. *The most effective and priceless type of treatment is journaling, which will improve your ability to think properly, comprehend who you are, and make sense of your life.*
12. *When you seek out new experiences rather than goods, you become rich in a different way.*
13. *The ability to pay attention with clarity is the most valuable skill in today's digital-first world, and daily meditation is the best method to develop it.*
14. *The formula for financial success is straightforward: Develop sound money-management skills, acquire marketable abilities, and produce more than you consume.*
15. *You are a lifelong student of life. Your only goal should be to continue learning, growing, and broadening your mind.*
16. *Fear is there to show you that you are interested and caring, not to stop you. Embrace your fear as a friend rather than battling it, for the second time you face something frightening, the initial encounter becomes almost inconsequential.*

17. *Before anyone else will, you must believe in yourself. That serves as the foundation for true confidence.*
18. *Life's best and most beautiful things, such as nature, laughter, kindness, love, and self-compassion, are imperfect and unrestricted.*
19. *We can only observe a star's brightness at the darkest hours: failure and hardship are the best instructors.*
20. *Keep an open mind, ask questions about everything, and make requests for what you want. When you live with such a mentality, you understand that doors always open after they close.*
21. *Playing the rapid, short-game yields tiny gains, whereas playing the sequential, long-game and giving oneself room to develop yields significant gains. Therefore, be hasty in your actions but patient in your outcomes.*
22. *The ability to think changes the game. You create it by deliberately concentrating on the things you control (your inputs and outputs) and disregarding what you don't (your outcomes).*
23. *Being where you are and doing all you can to help people and advance society is your purpose in life. When you perceive purpose from that perspective, you'll realize that your aim should not be to pursue your passions but to wholeheartedly follow your purpose.*
24. *You experience numerous lives simultaneously rather than just one, as you navigate the intricate tapestry of interconnected relationships and roles that shape your existence.*
25. *The people you share your life with make it meaningful to live. Make time for the people you love and surround yourself with positive individuals who inspire you.*
26. *You will live free from fear and regret if you keep an open mind and behave like an artist, yet think, make mistakes, and learn from them like a scientist.*
27. *If you can drop anything from your world, drop the ego. And if you can be anything in this world, be kind.*
28. *Truthfully, nobody cares what you do because we're all dealing with our issues. Therefore, stop demeaning yourself and start being authentic.*
29. *Money comes and goes in life, but time only flows one way. What you choose to do with your time today is the only thing you can control.*
30. *Ask for guidance but be astute enough to recognize whom to ask for it from.*

31. *Self-acceptance and self-awareness are the seeds of self-love. And the only road to all three is solitude since you can't look inside yourself in any other setting.*
32. *Amidst the noise of the outside world attempting to define you, taking time to contemplate and listen becomes essential to truly understand your authentic self.*
33. *Your perception of beauty and life's generosity, and your level of happiness will all increase as you express gratitude.*
34. *Since the quality of your thoughts directly affects the reality you experience, life is what you make of it.*

The biggest lesson you will learn is the power of resilience. Life is filled with unexpected challenges and setbacks, and it is through resilience that you can persevere and grow. Resilience will teach you that setbacks are not permanent and that you can overcome obstacles and emerge even more substantial with determination and a positive mindset. It will show you the importance of adapting to change, learning from failures, and maintaining a sense of hope and optimism. The lesson of resilience will be transformative, reminding you that you have the inner strength and resourcefulness to navigate life's ups and downs and continue moving forward with endurance as your guiding force.

Question #26

What advice do you wish you had taken years ago?

    Throughout life, we are constantly learning, yet there are some things we wish we had understood sooner. Some common forms of advice that will resonate regardless of how old you are or where you are in life are as follows:

1. *You will only be able to please some.*
2. *Stop putting off problems.*
3. *Be patient – don't expect immediate results.*
4. *Speak up more.*
5. *Don't be afraid of failure.*
6. *Discipline your mind.*
7. *Be open and flexible.*
8. *Never take people or things for granted.*

Thinking back, there may be one form of advice you wish you had taken years ago: to embrace failure and learn from it. In the past, you may have viewed failure as a reflection of your abilities or worth, which holds you back from taking risks and pursuing new opportunities. Had you embraced failure as a natural part of the learning process earlier on, you would have been more open to stepping out of your comfort zone and seizing chances for growth. Failure provides valuable lessons and insights that can lead to personal development and success. By reframing failure as an opportunity for growth and learning, you could have expanded your horizons and achieved more in various aspects of your life.

Sometimes we need to remember the value and importance of putting ourselves first. Remember to prioritize self-care and well-being. In the commotion of everyday life, it is easy to neglect self-care and put others' needs before our own. However, you will realize that self-care is not selfish but essential for overall well-being. Taking the time to recharge, engage in activities that bring joy, and nurture your physical and mental health will contribute to your happiness and resilience. By prioritizing self-care, you will better manage stress, avoid burnout, and foster a healthier work-life balance. It is always possible to start prioritizing self-care to establish healthier habits and enhance overall well-being.

This question evokes a profound sense of self-awareness and hindsight. It reminds me of missed opportunities and the wisdom that could have spared me from unnecessary struggles. In contemplating this, we acknowledge the value of listening to the guidance offered by others, drawing from their experiences and insights. It teaches the importance of humility and recognizing that seeking advice is not a sign of weakness but a courageous act of learning and growth. While we cannot change the past, this question serves as a powerful reminder to be open to guidance and wiser in heeding the lessons that come our way, ultimately shaping a more fulfilling and purposeful journey moving forward.

Question #27

What advice would you give your younger self?

Be kinder to yourself!

We are frequently our own worst critics. When stressed or angry, we speak to ourselves more critically than we would find appropriate for another person. We falsely believe that criticism inspires us to perform better. We intensify our tendency toward perfection. We raise our expectations for our conduct instead of speaking to ourselves with self-compassion to combat our uncertainty, apprehension, or annoyance.

You may handle difficult situations, including those you encounter and those you need to support others through. To use it effectively, follow these steps:

1) *Ask yourself what you need right now to give yourself a gentle and supportive nudge;*
2) *Use irreverence to challenge your beliefs;*
3) *reframe a trait or tendency to take a more balanced view;*

4) recognize your self-destructive tendencies;
5) borrow words from friends, quotes, or proverbs; and
6) write scripts for frequent scenarios.

A great word of advice to offer your younger self would be to embrace self-compassion and practice self-acceptance. In our younger years, we often held high standards and were overly critical of our perceived flaws and mistakes. It is vital to recognize that perfection is unattainable and that being kind to oneself in times of failure or self-doubt is essential. By cultivating self-compassion, you develop a healthier relationship with yourself, celebrating your strengths while acknowledging your areas for growth.

Another valuable piece of advice is prioritizing personal growth and pursuing passions without fear of judgment or comparison. It is easy to get caught up in societal expectations or the opinions of others, often leading to a sense of conformity or playing it safe. Instead, consider encouraging your younger self to explore interests, take risks, and follow *your* path, even if it diverges from the expectations of others. By nurturing personal growth and pursuing genuine passions, you foster a greater sense of fulfillment and authenticity in your journey.

Question #28

What advice would you give your future self?

      Contemplating advice you would give your future self leads you to envision the kind of person you aspire to become and the values you hold dear. You may encourage your future self to stay grounded in the present, cherishing each moment and embracing the journey, for life's beauty often lies in the small, fleeting details. You may remind yourself to be kind and compassionate, both to others and to yourself, as compassion is the cornerstone of building meaningful connections and fostering personal growth.

      Moreover, you may advise your future self to take risks and step out of your comfort zone, as it is through challenges and new experiences that you can truly discover your potential and expand the horizons of your understanding. You may urge your future self to always stay curious and open-minded, for in curiosity lies the gateway to continuous learning and the discovery of new passions. By noting these pieces of advice, you hope to shape a future that is filled with purpose, growth, and a sense of fulfillment.

Take this as an opportunity to reflect on the decisions you have previously made and speak to yourself as if you are writing a letter to yourself that you will read in a decade.

Remind yourself to develop a mindset that sees obstacles, restrictions, and failures as chances to try, learn, and advance. Be among individuals that inspire you. Remember to stay present and embrace the journey. It's easy to get caught up in the anticipation of the future or dwell on past experiences, but the true essence of life lies in the present moment. Remind your future self to savor each experience, embrace the ups and downs, and find joy in the simple pleasures. Life is a continuous journey of growth and discovery, and by staying present, you can fully immerse yourself in the richness of each moment and cultivate a more profound sense of gratitude and fulfillment.

Question #29

Is what you're doing right now making a difference in the world?

Have you ever wondered if your efforts are truly making an impact in the world? Are you still seeking to define what it means to make a difference? Rest assured, you are not alone in pondering these questions. Many individuals yearn to believe that their actions are shaping the world in positive ways, even though they may occasionally have unintended consequences. Making a difference entails influencing the world in which you live, and it is essential because it allows you to create the positive change you wish to see. Setting well-intentioned goals is a key element of happiness, as striving to have a positive impact on the things you value most can lead to a sense of fulfillment.

Your behavior and deeds have a direct impact on the people around you, and choosing kindness and compassion can greatly benefit those you interact with, as well as your own mental well-being. Even small acts of consideration and giving back to your community can create a ripple effect that extends far beyond your immediate surroundings, making a significant difference in the world. Whether through volunteering, contributing to causes, or supporting advocacy groups, there are various ways to extend your influence on local, national, and even international levels. Embracing these suggestions can empower you to make a meaningful and lasting impact on the world and the lives of others. Consider the following:

1. *Think about the matters most important to you and have been for a while.*
2. *Think about the areas of your life where you already have an impact.*
3. *Decide whether and where you could invest additional time and effort.*
4. *Make a move.*

Reflecting on whether what you're doing right now is making a difference prompts you to examine the impact of your actions and choices. In addition, it reminds you to evaluate whether your current pursuits align with your values and goals. Making a difference can take various forms, from contributing to a more significant cause to positively influencing the lives of those around you. By assessing the significance and potential ripple effects of your current actions, you can ensure that you are actively engaging in meaningful endeavors and maximizing your potential to create a positive impact in your own life and the lives of others.

Question #30

What is your next goal?

The question "What is your next goal?" holds great importance as it provides direction, motivation, and a sense of purpose. Setting personal goals helps to create a roadmap for self-improvement and growth. By identifying the next personal goal, you can channel your energy and resources towards a specific objective, bringing clarity and focus to your life. Whether advancing in your career, improving a skill, nurturing relationships, or enhancing your well-being, having a clear goal allows you to prioritize your actions and make conscious decisions that align with your aspirations.

Personal goals act as catalysts for personal development and growth. They push you outside your comfort zone and encourage you to challenge yourself, acquire new knowledge, and develop essential skills. Pursuing a personal goal provides opportunities for learning, self-discovery, and overcoming obstacles. It fosters resilience, determination, and a sense of achievement. Working towards a personal goal gives you valuable experiences and insights that contribute to your growth.

Having a personal goal brings a sense of fulfillment and satisfaction. When you have a clear objective and make progress towards it, you experience a sense of accomplishment and purpose. It gives you a sense of direction and drives you to strive for continuous improvement. Pursuing personal goals allows you to tap into your potential, unlock new possibilities, and live a more fulfilling life. It reminds you that you are in control of your destiny and have the power to shape your future. Overall, this question empowers you to embrace growth, find purpose, and live a life of intention and fulfillment.

Question #31

Are you doing everything you can to achieve your goals?

      Whether you are doing everything you can to achieve your goals is a powerful question that compels you to evaluate your commitment and effort. It serves as a reminder to take ownership of your actions and ensure you are fully dedicated to pursuing your aspirations. By assessing your commitment, resource-utilization, and proactive mindset, you can identify areas for improvement and make necessary adjustments to ensure that you are giving your best. This question motivates you to overcome obstacles, push beyond your limits, and actively strive for success in pursuing your goals.

      Answering this question requires a deep self-analysis and examination of your habits, mindset, and actions. It compels you to evaluate whether you are utilizing your time, resources, and talents effectively and efficiently. It pushes you to challenge any self-imposed limitations or excuses that may hinder your progress. By holding yourself accountable and striving to do everything within your power to achieve your goals, you are more likely to overcome obstacles, persevere through setbacks, and make meaningful strides toward realizing your aspirations.

Furthermore, this question highlights the importance of self-motivation and a growth mindset. It encourages you to continuously seek opportunities for improvement, learn from failures, and embrace a proactive and resilient approach toward your goals. You can maintain a sense of urgency, focus, and determination by constantly assessing whether you are doing everything you can. It encourages you to explore innovative strategies, seek guidance and support when needed, and push beyond your comfort zone. Ultimately, this question is a compass for your personal and professional development, driving you to strive for excellence and maximize your potential.

Question #32

What is holding you back from achieving your dreams?

With this question, I encourage you to reflect on any potential limitations, self-doubt, or external factors impeding your progress. Identifying these challenges can help you develop strategies to overcome them and pursue your dreams with determination and perseverance. Remember that setbacks and obstacles are a natural part of any journey, and with resilience and a proactive mindset, you can work toward overcoming them and progressing towards your goals.

First, self-limiting beliefs and fear of failure can be significant barriers. These doubts and negative thoughts can undermine your confidence and prevent you from taking necessary risks or pursuing ambitious goals. Overcoming these mental barriers requires cultivating a growth mindset, challenging limiting beliefs, and embracing resilience and self-belief.

Second, a lack of clear goals or a well-defined plan can hinder progress. With a clear vision or roadmap, making focused and purposeful strides toward your dreams becomes more accessible. Setting specific, achievable goals and breaking them down into actionable steps helps create a sense of direction and momentum. The key word here is achievable, as sometimes we set the bar too high and set ourselves up for failure. Developing a strategic plan with measurable objectives and timelines enables you to track progress and make necessary adjustments.

Finally, external factors such as potentially limited resources, support, or opportunities can present obstacles. However, it is crucial to recognize that resourcefulness and adaptability are essential. Seeking to expand networks and proactively creating opportunities can help overcome these challenges. It is also crucial to surround yourself with a supportive network of individuals who believe in you and your dreams, as their encouragement and guidance can provide the necessary motivation and assistance to move forward.

By reflecting on these potential barriers, you can take proactive steps to overcome them, whether it involves shifting your mindset, refining your goals and plans, or seeking the necessary resources and support. It reminds you that you have the willpower and capability to overcome obstacles and work toward achieving your dreams.

Question #33

If you had all the free time in the world, what would you do with it?

This question evokes a sense of exploration and possibility. Here are some possibilities to consider:

First, prioritize activities that foster personal growth and learning. You could dedicate time to delve deeper into your interests and passions, whether pursuing further education, engaging in creative endeavors, or exploring new hobbies. Having ample free time would allow you to invest in self-improvement and expand your knowledge and skills.

Second or next, you could focus on nurturing relationships and connecting with loved ones. With ample free time, you could cherish the opportunity to spend quality time with family and friends, strengthening those bonds and creating lasting memories. You could prioritize meaningful conversations, shared experiences, and making a sense of belonging and connection. Cultivating and enriching relationships will bring joy, support, and a sense of fulfillment to your life.

Finally, you could embrace the beauty of travel and exploration. With unlimited free time, you would embark on adventures worldwide, immersing yourself in different cultures, landscapes, and experiences. You could seek diverse destinations, engage in local communities, and broaden your horizons. Travel would provide an opportunity for personal growth, expanding your perspectives and deepening your understanding of the world and its inhabitants.

If you had all the free time in the world, would you choose to focus on personal growth, nurturing relationships, and embracing the wonders of travel? Or would you fill the time with meaningless relationships and activities? Your response to this question will allow you to reflect on self-discovery, connection, priorities and exploration.

Question #34

After thinking about your answer to Question #33, why aren't you making time for those things now?

      How you respond to this question will vary depending on your answer to Question #33. Since you are reading this book, your central focus is naturally on self-growth. The challenge of making time for self-growth stems from various factors. Firstly, the fast-paced nature of modern life often prioritizes productivity and external obligations over personal development. Work demands, family responsibilities, and social commitments can leave little time and energy for self-reflection and growth. In addition, the societal pressure to constantly be busy and productive can create a mindset that views self-growth as a luxury rather than a necessity.

      Secondly, the fear of stepping out of our comfort zones can hinder our willingness to make time for self-growth. Self-growth often requires embracing change, taking risks, and confronting personal limitations. This can evoke vulnerability and uncertainty, leading to resistance or avoidance. The familiarity of our comfort zones can provide a false sense of security, making it challenging to prioritize self-growth amidst the fear of the unknown.

Lastly, a lack of awareness or clarity about self-growth's benefits may contribute to not reflecting and devoting enough time. Without understanding the profound positive impact of self-growth on our overall well-being, fulfillment, and success, it becomes easier to overlook its importance. The value of self-growth lies in its long-term benefits, such as increased self-awareness, improved skills, enhanced resilience, and a more profound sense of purpose. However, recognizing and internalizing these benefits is necessary to prioritize self-growth amidst the competing demands of daily life.

Recognizing the significance and prioritizing self-growth is essential. This involves valuing personal development as a fundamental aspect of a fulfilling and meaningful life. It requires creating intentional space in our schedules, setting clear goals, and committing to investing in our growth. By shifting our mindset, embracing discomfort, and acknowledging the long-term benefits of self-growth, we can overcome the barriers that prevent us from making time for self-growth and unlocking our full potential.

Question #35

If you had all the money in the world, what would you do with it?

If you answered this question by focusing on purchasing luxury items, perhaps you're going to want to think about your priorities and how you define happiness. As you reflect deeper, this question triggers thoughts of abundance, possibilities, and the potential for positive impact. Some things to consider when reflecting on this question:

Firstly, you could prioritize making a difference in the lives of others and contributing to causes that align with your values. You could invest in philanthropic initiatives, support organizations working towards social and environmental change, and provide resources to empower needy communities. By leveraging your financial resources, you could create a more equitable and sustainable world where everyone can access opportunities and a higher quality of life.

Secondly, you could focus on personal growth and experiences that enrich your life and expand your horizons. You could invest in lifelong learning, exploring different cultures, and pursuing meaningful experiences. Traveling to diverse destinations, immersing yourself in new environments, and engaging in transformative experiences broaden your perspectives, foster personal development, and deepen your understanding of the world. You could also prioritize nurturing relationships, spending quality time with loved ones, and creating memorable moments that bring joy and fulfillment.

Lastly, you could invest in innovation and research to address pressing global challenges. You could support scientific advancements, technological innovations, and breakthroughs in healthcare, renewable energy, and environmental conservation. By allocating resources towards research and development, you could contribute to finding sustainable solutions to complex problems and drive progress towards a better future for all.

If you had all the money in the world, you could strive to impact society positively, prioritize personal growth and meaningful experiences, and invest in innovation and research. The abundance of financial resources would be leveraged to create a more just and sustainable world while fostering personal growth and advancing transformative initiatives.

Question #36

Do you believe money equals happiness?

The question of whether money equals happiness is a complex question. While money can contribute to certain aspects of happiness, such as providing security, comfort, and access to opportunities, it does not guarantee overall happiness. Research has shown that additional wealth does not necessarily lead to a proportional increase in happiness beyond a certain threshold that covers basic needs. Personal relationships, a sense of purpose, and emotional well-being are crucial in determining one's happiness.

Happiness is a multidimensional concept encompassing various aspects of life, including physical and mental health, social connections, personal fulfillment, and meaning. While financial resources can facilitate some aspects of happiness, such as meeting basic needs and pursuing one's interests, they alone cannot fulfill all the components that contribute to true happiness. For example, psychological well-being, life satisfaction, and a sense of purpose are often derived from experiences, relationships, personal growth, and a meaningful connection with the world around us.

Ultimately, the belief that money equals happiness can be limiting and misleading. It is essential to recognize the importance of balancing material wealth with other aspects of well-being. Cultivating solid relationships, pursuing personal passions, maintaining good health, and fostering a positive mindset is equally, if not more, essential for long-lasting happiness. While money can enhance certain aspects of life, the holistic approach to well-being genuinely contributes to genuine and sustainable happiness.

Question #37

What would you do if you had all the resources in the world not to fail?

  Contemplating the idea of having all the resources in the world to never fail evokes a thrilling sense of boundless possibilities and potential. In such a scenario, you would embark on audacious ventures that might seem unattainable in the absence of resources. You could fearlessly pursue your passions, exploring uncharted territories, and pushing the boundaries of your capabilities. With unlimited resources at your disposal, you would be driven to tackle grand challenges, not solely for personal gain but to make a positive and transformative impact on the world. The absence of fear of failure would liberate you from hesitations and doubts, allowing you to take risks and embrace innovation with unwavering confidence. Your endeavors would be guided by a deep sense of purpose, channeling the abundance of resources towards uplifting communities, fostering education, and promoting environmental sustainability. While such a scenario may be a mere dream, the inspiration it brings will fuel your determination to make a difference with the resources available to you, no matter how limited they may be.

  The question of what you would do if you had all the resources not to fail sparks a sense of boundless opportunity and potential. With unlimited resources, you can embark on ambitious endeavors that align with your passions and values.

If you had all the resources not to fail, your potential actions would be virtually limitless. With unlimited resources, you could embark on ambitious projects and initiatives that align with your passions and values. You could tackle significant global challenges such as poverty, climate change, or healthcare accessibility by investing in innovative solutions, research, and infrastructure. You could establish foundations or organizations to support and drive positive change on a large scale.

Furthermore, you could revolutionize industries and technologies by funding cutting-edge research and development. You could lead scientific breakthroughs, advance renewable energy solutions, or promote advancements in medicine, space exploration, or artificial intelligence. By harnessing your resources effectively, you could accelerate progress and push the boundaries of what is currently possible.

You could prioritize humanitarian efforts, supporting needy communities, and facilitating sustainable development. You could invest in education, healthcare, and infrastructure in underserved regions, empowering individuals and promoting equality of opportunity. You could create platforms and networks to foster collaboration and knowledge exchange, bringing together experts and visionaries from various disciplines to collectively address complex global issues.

The possibilities for someone with unlimited resources to not fail are vast. You could make transformative contributions globally, to a sustainable and prosperous future. However, it is essential to recognize the importance of responsible and ethical use of resources and consider the diverse perspectives and needs of those affected by their actions.

Question #38

How important are your goals to you?

      Goals are vital in our lives as they provide direction, motivation, and a sense of purpose. They give us something to strive for and work towards, whether in our personal lives, relationships, careers, or other areas. Goals help us clarify our desires and set a path for growth and achievement. They provide structure and focus, enabling us to prioritize our time, energy, and resources effectively. Moreover, goals challenge us to step out of our comfort zones, overcome obstacles, and develop new skills and abilities. By setting and pursuing meaningful goals, we can experience a sense of fulfillment, accomplishment, and continuous growth, ultimately leading to a more purposeful and satisfying life.

      The importance of your goals should be a paramount consideration. They serve as guiding beacons that provide direction, motivation, and purpose in your life. Goals give you a sense of clarity and focus, helping you to prioritize your actions and make conscious choices aligned with your aspirations. In addition, they serve as markers of personal growth and achievement, pushing you to strive for progress and excellence continually.

Your goals are not merely fleeting desires; they represent the values and ideals that you hold dear. They reflect on your most profound personal and professional aspirations and encompass various aspects of your life, such as relationships, career, health, and personal development. Each goal holds significance to you, as they represent the vision of the future you desire and the person you aspire to become.

Your goals are not isolated pursuits; they are interconnected and intertwined with your overall sense of fulfillment and well-being. Achieving your goals brings profound satisfaction, contentment, and purpose. In addition, they inspire you to overcome obstacles, embrace challenges, and grow as an individual.

Question #39

What is the number one priority in your life right now?

The number one priority in your life should be personal well-being. Unfortunately, in our fast-paced and demanding world, it's easy to neglect self-care and prioritize external obligations over our physical, mental, and emotional health. Recognizing the importance of self-care, you will prioritize activities that nourish and rejuvenate you; this includes maintaining a balanced lifestyle, practicing mindfulness and self-reflection, engaging in regular exercise, and fostering healthy relationships. By prioritizing your well-being, you can show up as the best version of yourself in all areas of your life.

Personal growth and self-improvement should also be high on your list of priorities. Continual learning and development are essential for leading a fulfilling and meaningful life. Whether it's acquiring new skills, expanding your knowledge base, or challenging yourself to step outside your comfort zone, dedicating yourself to personal growth brings forth positive changes. This involves seeking out opportunities for self-improvement, such as reading books, attending workshops, or pursuing further education. By investing in your personal development, you can continually evolve and unlock your full potential.

Lastly, encouraging and nurturing meaningful relationships should be another top priority. Recognize the profound impact of solid and authentic connections on our overall well-being and happiness. Prioritize spending quality time with loved ones, fostering open communication, and showing support and care for those who matter most to you. By prioritizing relationships, you aim to create a supportive and nurturing network that brings joy, love, and a sense of belonging to your life.

The number one priority in your life right now should be YOU!

Question #40

What actions are you actively taking to in your response to Question #39?

Whether or not you responded with prioritizing yourself and your needs in the previous question, prioritizing yourself in life is essential for nurturing your well-being, fostering personal growth, and ultimately leading a fulfilling and balanced existence.

To actively prioritize yourself, you can take several actions that foster self-care and well-being.

Firstly, setting boundaries is essential. This involves learning to say no when necessary and creating space for activities that rejuvenate and nourish you. Establishing healthy boundaries with people around you can prevent burnout and allocate time and energy to prioritize your needs and desires.

Secondly, practicing self-care rituals regularly is crucial. This may involve engaging in activities that bring you joy and relaxation, such as practicing mindfulness, exercising, reading, or engaging in creative pursuits. Carving out dedicated time for self-care allows you to recharge, reduce stress, and maintain a healthy balance in your life.

Practicing mindfulness is the art of being fully present and aware in the present moment, without judgment or distraction. It involves attentively observing our thoughts, emotions, and sensations while embracing the richness of the current experience. By cultivating mindfulness, we learn to acknowledge and accept the reality of each moment, empowering us to respond thoughtfully rather than react impulsively to life's challenges. This heightened awareness enables us to break free from the past or worries about the future, bringing us back to the tranquility and clarity of the here and now. Mindfulness is a powerful tool to reduce stress, enhance mental focus, and deepen our connection with ourselves and the world around us. As we practice mindfulness, we embark on a transformative journey of self-discovery, fostering compassion and gratitude and savoring the profound richness of life's simplest moments.

Furthermore, nurturing a positive mindset and cultivating self-compassion are vital. You can actively engage in practices such as gratitude journaling, affirmations, or seeking support from a therapist or coach. You can enhance your overall well-being and resilience by fostering a positive internal dialogue and treating yourself with kindness and understanding.

Prioritizing yourself requires setting boundaries, practicing self-care rituals, and cultivating a positive mindset. These actions empower you to prioritize your well-being, ensure a healthy balance in life, and create a foundation of self-care that supports your overall happiness and fulfillment. By actively taking these steps, you can maintain your physical, mental, and emotional health, enabling you to show up as the best version of yourself in all areas of your life.

Question #41

Does your current job make you happy?

       This question is an essential consideration for overall well-being and fulfillment. Happiness in a job is influenced by various factors, including job satisfaction, completion of one's passions and values, work-life balance, and positive relationships with colleagues. While/when reflecting on your current job, you assess whether it aligns with your interests, provides growth opportunities, and contributes to a sense of purpose.

       If your current job brings you joy, fulfillment, and a sense of accomplishment, it significantly can contribute to your happiness. It becomes a source of motivation and enthusiasm, making the work enjoyable. Positive relationships with coworkers, a supportive work environment, and personal and professional development opportunities also significantly influence job satisfaction and happiness.

However, if your current job does not align with your passions, values, or long-term goals, it may impact your happiness and well-being. Therefore, evaluating whether your job provides a sense of purpose and fulfillment or feels like a repetitive routine is crucial. If you consistently feel unhappy or unfulfilled, exploring other options that align better with your aspirations and values might be worth exploring.

Finding happiness in a job is a highly individual and subjective experience. It requires self-reflection, honesty, and a willingness to make necessary changes. Therefore, regular assessment of job satisfaction and alignment with personal goals and values is crucial for ensuring that your work contributes positively to your overall happiness and well-being.

Question #42

Is your current career one you would ultimately pick if you could start all over again?

Reflecting on whether your current career is one you would ultimately choose if you could start all over again brings to light a complex mix of emotions and considerations. You may have certain regrets or wonder "what if" about other paths not taken; it is essential to approach this question with a sense of perspective and acceptance of where you are in your journey.

You likely find your current career fulfilling, challenging, and consisting of rewarding aspects. Acknowledging and appreciating those aspects as they contribute to your growth and personal development is essential. Additionally, the skills and experiences you have gained are valuable assets that have shaped you professionally and personally.

However, contemplating alternative career paths can also reveal dissatisfaction or unfulfilled desires. Questioning if other paths align more closely with your passions, values, or long-term goals is natural. This reflection can be an opportunity to reassess your priorities, consider potential changes or adjustments, and explore new possibilities within your current career or beyond.

Ultimately, the answer to whether your current career is the one you would choose if starting over is a profoundly personal one. It involves evaluating your values, aspirations, and sense of fulfillment. It is vital to approach this reflection with self-compassion, recognizing that life is a continuous journey of growth and learning. Regardless of the outcome, self-reflection can guide you toward making intentional choices that align with your authentic self and lead to a career path that brings you fulfillment and happiness.

This question serves as a powerful catalyst for introspection, compelling you to delve into the core of your career choices. It invites contemplation on the alignment of your current path with personal passions, values, and aspirations, while also encouraging a reassessment of the impact of external influences and the wisdom of hindsight. Ultimately, this question prompts you to not only evaluate your present satisfaction but also to envision a future that resonates more authentically with your true desires and potential.

Question #43

Does your diet make you feel the best you can?

Diet is not just about what we eat; it encompasses a broader perspective that includes our overall relationship with food, people and lifestyle choices. It considers how we approach eating, our mindset, our eating patterns, and the context in which we consume meals. It also acknowledges the importance of portion control, mindful eating, hydration, regular physical activity, and adequate rest. By recognizing that diet encompasses these multifaceted aspects, we can develop a more holistic approach to nourishing our bodies and promoting overall well-being.

The impact of your diet on how you feel is a significant consideration for your overall well-being and quality of life. Reflecting on whether your current diet makes you feel the best you can involves assessing the balance of nutrients, the impact on your energy levels, digestion, mental clarity, and overall physical health.

If your diet consists of nourishing, whole foods that provide diverse nutrients, it can positively impact your well-being. For example, a diet rich in fruits, vegetables, lean proteins, whole grains, and healthy fats can provide the necessary fuel for your body and support optimal functioning. When you consciously prioritize nutrient-dense foods and listen to your body's signals, you can experience increased energy levels, improved digestion, enhanced mental focus, and overall vitality.

On the other hand, if your diet is primarily composed of processed foods, excessive sugars, unhealthy fats, or lacking essential nutrients, it can lead to feelings of lethargy, sluggishness, and poor overall health. In such cases, it becomes crucial to reevaluate your dietary choices and adjust to better support your well-being.

This question goes beyond the mere consumption of food; it encompasses the broader concept of nourishment in our lives. While the nutritional aspect is undoubtedly crucial, it also compels us to consider the overall environment we immerse ourselves in and the people we surround ourselves with. Our emotional and mental diet, so to speak, can have just as significant an impact on our well-being as the food we eat. Negative relationships, toxic environments, and stress-inducing situations can all contribute to feelings of unease and discomfort, ultimately affecting our overall sense of wellness.

In this holistic view of diet, we recognize that the people we associate with and the environments we inhabit play a pivotal role in shaping our well-being. Positive, supportive relationships can provide emotional sustenance, just as a nourishing meal can provide physical sustenance. Conversely, negative or toxic relationships can drain us of our vitality, much like consuming unhealthy food can lead to physical discomfort. The question challenges us to evaluate not only what we eat but also the broader aspects of our lives, prompting us to seek balance and harmony in our overall diet for optimal well-being. In essence, it encourages us to curate our lives with the same care and mindfulness that we apply to our food choices, recognizing that true health and happiness are the product of a holistic approach to nourishment.

Reflecting on your diet allows you to be mindful of what you consume and how it impacts your body and mind. It encourages you to make informed choices, prioritize whole and nutrient-dense foods, and establish a balanced and sustainable approach to eating. By regularly reassessing and adapting your diet, you can strive to find a way of eating that truly makes you feel your best and supports your overall health and well-being.

Question #44

Is there something you are avoiding? Is it time to let it go?

    Reflecting on whether there is something you are avoiding can reveal hidden tensions or unresolved issues that may be holding you back from personal growth and happiness. Avoidance can stem from fear, discomfort, or a desire to protect yourself from emotional pain or uncertainty. It could be a challenging conversation, a difficult decision, or a lingering task you have been putting off. Acknowledging what you are avoiding requires self-honesty and a willingness to confront uncomfortable truths.

    Once you identify what you are avoiding, evaluating whether it is time to let it go becomes essential. Letting go can be a powerful act of self-empowerment and liberation. It involves releasing attachments to outcomes, old beliefs, or toxic relationships that no longer serve you. First, however, it is essential to discern whether letting go is the best course of action or if it requires a different approach, such as confronting the issue directly or seeking support from others.

When faced with a challenging situation, there are different ways to respond. One option is to let go, which can bring relief from stress, but might also leave issues unresolved. Another approach is confronting the problem directly, which can lead to resolution and personal growth, but might also lead to conflict. Seeking support from others is another choice, offering fresh perspectives and validation, but it could also lead to dependency or conflicting advice. The right choice depends on the situation, your values, and your well-being, and sometimes a combination of these approaches might be best.

The decision to let go or confront what you are avoiding requires careful consideration and self-reflection. It involves weighing each option's potential benefits and drawbacks and listening to your intuition. Letting go can create space for new opportunities, personal growth, and emotional healing. However, it is crucial to approach this process with compassion for oneself and recognize that letting go is a gradual and ongoing journey.

Question #45

*What limiting beliefs are you holding on to?
Is it time to break them?*

      Reflecting on the limiting beliefs you are holding on to can be a transformative exercise that helps you uncover self-imposed barriers that hinder your growth and potential. Limiting beliefs are deeply ingrained notions about ourselves, others, or the world that restrict our possibilities and create self-doubt. Identifying these beliefs requires introspection and a willingness to challenge long-held assumptions.

      Once you become aware of your limiting beliefs, it is essential to question their validity and consider whether it is time to break free from them. These beliefs often stem from past experiences, societal conditioning, or fear of failure. However, they prevent you from fully embracing your capabilities, pursuing opportunities, or taking risks. Breaking free from limiting beliefs involves cultivating a growth mindset, embracing self-compassion, and adopting empowering ideas that support your potential and resilience.

You can unlock new personal and professional growth opportunities by challenging and dismantling limiting beliefs. It requires a commitment to self-reflection, self-compassion, and a willingness to step outside your comfort zone. As you let go of limiting beliefs, you create space for self-confidence, creativity, and a greater sense of fulfillment. Breaking free from these beliefs empowers you to pursue your dreams, embrace new challenges, and live a life aligned with your true potential.

Limiting beliefs are negative thoughts or ideas that can hinder personal growth, success, and well-being. Here are some common forms of limiting beliefs:

1. **Self-Doubt**: Believing that you're not capable or competent enough to achieve your goals. This can lead to a lack of confidence and avoidance of challenges.

2. **Perfectionism**: Thinking that everything must be flawless or perfect, which can create fear of failure and hinder progress due to the unrealistic standards set.

3. **Fear of Rejection**: Believing that others will reject or criticize you, leading to hesitancy in expressing yourself or pursuing opportunities.

4. **Scarcity Mindset**: Believing that there's not enough to go around, leading to feelings of competition and an inability to see abundance and opportunities.

5. **Imposter Syndrome**: Feeling like a fraud despite evidence of your accomplishments, leading to self-sabotage and downplaying achievements.

6. **Catastrophizing**: Expecting the worst outcome in every situation, which can increase anxiety and prevent you from taking necessary risks.

7. **Fixed Mindset**: Believing that your abilities and intelligence are fixed traits, leading to avoidance of challenges that might challenge your self-perception.

8. **Comparison**: Constantly measuring yourself against others and feeling inadequate, which can erode self-esteem and motivation.

9. **Victim Mentality**: Believing that external factors have complete control over your life, leading to a sense of powerlessness and lack of responsibility for your own choices.

10. **All-or-Nothing Thinking**: Seeing situations as either entirely good or entirely bad, leading to missed opportunities and an inability to see nuanced solutions.

11. **Labeling**: Defining yourself based on mistakes or failures, which can lead to a negative self-identity and reluctance to try new things.

12. **Overgeneralization**: Drawing broad conclusions from isolated incidents, leading to self-limiting beliefs based on limited evidence.

Identifying and challenging these limiting beliefs is crucial for personal development. Developing a growth mindset, practicing self-compassion, seeking evidence to dispute negative thoughts, and reframing challenges as learning opportunities can help counteract these beliefs and foster a more positive and empowered outlook.

Question #46

What are your daily bad habits? Your weaknesses?

Reflecting on your daily bad habits and weaknesses allows you to gain insight into areas where you may be delaying your progress or experiencing recurring challenges. Identifying these habits requires honesty and self-awareness; we all have places to improve. By acknowledging and addressing these weaknesses, you can work towards personal growth and develop strategies to overcome them.

One of your daily bad habits may be procrastination, where you put off important tasks or activities until the last minute. This habit can lead to increased stress and decreased productivity. Another weakness could be a tendency to succumb to distractions, such as spending excessive time on social media or engaging in unproductive activities. These distractions can deter your ability to focus and efficiently use your time.

To address these weaknesses, you can adopt strategies like setting clear goals, breaking tasks into smaller, manageable steps, and creating a structured schedule. Additionally, practicing self-discipline and implementing techniques like time-blocking and removing distractions can help you stay on track. Building new, positive habits such as prioritizing essential tasks, setting deadlines, and practicing mindfulness can also contribute to overcoming these weaknesses.

Recognizing and actively working on your daily bad habits and weaknesses is a continuous process. It requires self-reflection, commitment, and a willingness to make changes. By consciously addressing these areas, you can enhance your effectiveness, boost your productivity, and cultivate a healthier and more balanced lifestyle.

Question #47

What are your daily good habits? Your strengths?

  Reflecting on your daily good habits and strengths is an opportunity to acknowledge the positive aspects of your character and routines that contribute to your well-being and success. In addition, these habits and strengths play a crucial role in shaping your actions, attitudes, and overall fulfillment.

  A possible daily good habit is practicing gratitude. Taking a few moments each day to express appreciation for the things and people in your life fosters a positive mindset and helps you find joy in the present moment. Another strength could be adequate time-management, where you prioritize tasks, set realistic goals, and allocate your time efficiently. This lets you stay organized, meet deadlines, and maintain a healthy work-life balance.

Other strengths may include resilience, adaptability, and staying focused in challenging situations. These qualities allow you to navigate obstacles, bounce back from setbacks, and remain committed to your goals. Another strength is actively seeking opportunities for personal growth and continuous learning. Engaging in activities such as reading, taking courses, or pursuing new skills expands your knowledge and keeps you motivated and intellectually stimulated.

Recognizing and appreciating these daily good habits and strengths empowers you to build upon them and leverage them in various aspects of your life. Maximizing these positive attributes can enhance personal and professional growth, foster stronger relationships, and navigate life's challenges confidently and resiliently. In addition, continuously nurturing these habits and strengths allows you to live a more purposeful and fulfilling life.

Question #48

What is the biggest thing holding you back right now from making changes in your life?

       This question requires deeply exploring your inner thoughts, fears, and patterns. Identifying and understanding the underlying factors preventing you from taking the necessary steps toward positive change is essential. There are four main reasons why people choose to change:

    1) *People change when they hurt enough that they have to.*
    2) *People change when they see enough that they are inspired to.*
    3) *People change when they learn enough that they want to.*
    4) *People change when they receive enough that they are able to.*

       One significant factor that may be holding you back is the fear of failure or the fear of the unknown. This is a common theme in this book. This fear can create a sense of uncertainty and hesitation, making it difficult to embrace change and take risks. However, it is crucial to recognize that failure is a natural part of growth and that stepping out of your comfort zone is essential for personal development.

Another factor that may hinder progress is a need for self-belief or self-confidence. Doubts and negative self-talk can undermine your belief in your abilities and limit your willingness to act. Building self-confidence and cultivating a positive mindset can help overcome this obstacle, allowing you to approach change with courage and determination.

Additionally, external factors such as the influence of others or societal expectations can contribute to the resistance to making changes. For example, the fear of judgment or the pressure to conform to certain norms can create barriers to personal growth. Therefore, it is crucial to differentiate between external expectations and your values and desires and to have the courage to follow your path.

When contemplating this question, it's crucial to recognize that change is a fundamental aspect of personal growth and adaptation. People may need to make changes in their lives for various reasons. Change can be prompted by a desire for self-improvement, a response to external circumstances, or an acknowledgment of personal dissatisfaction or unfulfilled goals. It often emerges from the recognition that staying stagnant can lead to complacency, missed opportunities, or even a decline in overall well-being.

Signs that change may be necessary can manifest in numerous ways. People may include feelings of restlessness or discontent, a sense of unfulfillment in one's current circumstances, persistent stress or anxiety, or a recognition that current habits or behaviors are not conducive to long-term happiness and success. External factors such as changes in one's environment, career, or relationships can also serve as catalysts for change. Ultimately, change is a natural and necessary part of life, driven by our innate drive for personal growth and the ever-evolving nature of our world. Therefore, when addressing what holds someone back from making changes, it's vital to consider these broader motivations and the signs that may signal the need for transformation in one's life.

By identifying and acknowledging these factors, you can take proactive steps to address them and create a mindset that is open to change. This may involve seeking support from trusted individuals, setting realistic goals, and challenging limiting beliefs. Of course, embracing change requires courage, resilience, and a commitment to personal growth. Still, by recognizing and addressing what is holding you back, you can empower yourself to make the necessary changes and move towards a more fulfilling and meaningful life.

Question #49

Is the environment you are currently living in healthy?

     Our environment plays a significant role in shaping our physical, mental, and emotional health. Therefore, evaluating whether the domain you are in is healthy involves considering various factors, such as the physical space, the social dynamics, and the overall atmosphere.

     Regarding the physical space, assessing if it promotes a sense of safety, comfort, and cleanliness is essential. A cluttered or disorganized environment can contribute to stress and make it challenging to focus and relax. Conversely, creating an organized and aesthetically pleasing space can enhance productivity, relaxation, and overall mental well-being.

     Furthermore, the social dynamics within the environment should be evaluated. Healthy relationships and positive social interactions are vital for our emotional well-being. It is essential to assess whether the people around you uplift and support you or if there are toxic dynamics that drain your energy and contribute to negativity. Surrounding yourself with individuals who encourage personal growth, respect boundaries, and foster a positive atmosphere is crucial for maintaining a healthy living environment.

Lastly, considering the overall atmosphere of the environment is essential. This includes noise levels, exposure to natural light, air quality, and access to nature. A peaceful, serene atmosphere can significantly impact your mood, concentration, and well-being.

If your current environment is not healthy, make changes or adjustments that may be necessary. This could involve decluttering and organizing your physical space, setting boundaries and/or eliminating toxic relationships, seeking support or therapy, or even considering a change of environment if feasible. Taking proactive steps to create a healthy living environment can profoundly affect your overall quality of life and contribute to a sense of harmony and well-being.

Question #50

Are you discussing your mental health?

  Whether or not you are discussing your mental health is a crucial aspect of self-awareness and personal well-being. Mental health plays a vital role in our overall quality of life, and open communication about our mental well-being is essential for destigmatization, support, and access to resources. Mental health constitutes a cornerstone of our holistic well-being, exerting a profound influence on the overall quality of our lives. Just as our physical health necessitates attention and care, our mental well-being equally demands acknowledgment and nurturing.

  The significance of mental health awareness is underscored by its far-reaching impact on our emotions, thoughts, behaviors, and relationships. Furthermore, it is incumbent upon us to foster an environment of open and candid dialogue surrounding mental well-being. Engaging in such discussions not only serves to dismantle the stigma often associated with mental health challenges but also facilitates the creation of a compassionate and understanding community. By normalizing conversations about mental health, we pave the way for individuals to seek help, receive support, and avail themselves of the resources necessary for their healing and growth.

If you are not discussing your mental health, it may be beneficial to evaluate the reasons behind it. It could be due to personal discomfort, fear of judgment, or societal pressure to appear strong and independent. However, recognizing the importance of mental health and the potential benefits of open discussions can motivate you to initiate conversations and seek the support you need. Prioritizing mental health discussions allows you to cultivate self-awareness, resilience, and emotional well-being, contributing to a healthier and more fulfilling life.

Discussing your mental health can involve reaching out to trusted individuals, such as friends, family, or mental health professionals, to share your thoughts, feelings, and concerns. In addition, it is essential to have a support system in place that can provide understanding, empathy, and guidance during challenging times. By engaging in conversations about mental health, you can gain valuable insights, receive emotional support, and explore potential strategies for self-care and healing.

Moreover, discussing mental health promotes awareness and understanding within society. By openly sharing our experiences and struggles, we contribute to breaking down the barriers and stereotypes surrounding mental health. These conversations can reduce stigma and encourage others to seek help and support when needed. Through dialogue and education, we can foster a more supportive and inclusive environment for mental health.

Question #51

Are you doing everything you can to maintain a healthy mind?

    Reflecting on whether you are doing everything you can to maintain a healthy mind is essential in self-evaluation and personal growth. A practical reason is for overall well-being, productivity, and a fulfilling life. In addition, assessing your current practices and habits allows you to identify areas of improvement and take proactive steps toward nurturing your mental health.

    Maintaining a healthy mind involves various factors, including self-care, stress management, emotional well-being, and personal growth. In addition, it requires you to prioritize activities that promote relaxation, such as practicing mindfulness, engaging in hobbies, getting regular exercise, and ensuring sufficient sleep. These activities help reduce stress, improve mood, and enhance cognitive function.

    Additionally, it is essential to cultivate emotional well-being by nurturing positive relationships, expressing emotions, and seeking support when needed. This includes engaging in open and honest communication, setting boundaries, and practicing self-compassion and self-acceptance. Seeking therapy or counseling can also be beneficial in developing effective coping mechanisms and gaining insights into personal challenges.

Furthermore, maintaining a healthy mind involves a commitment to lifelong learning and personal growth. Engaging in activities stimulating the mind, such as reading, learning new skills, or pursuing creative outlets, fosters intellectual and emotional well-being. It is also essential to be mindful of negative influences, such as excessive media consumption or comparison with others, and actively choosing to focus on positive and uplifting content.

Reflecting on whether you are doing everything you can to maintain a healthy mind allows you to identify areas of improvement and take proactive steps toward self-care and personal growth. It reminds you to prioritize your mental health, seek support when needed, and embrace practices that nourish your mind, body, and spirit. Investing in your mental well-being can cultivate resilience, enhance your overall quality of life, and thrive in all areas of your life.

Question #52

Are you living in the past or present?

　　　This critical inquiry helps you gain insight into your mindset and approach to life. Living in the past refers to dwelling on past experiences, regrets, or nostalgic memories, while living in the present means being fully engaged and aware of the current moment.

　　　Living in the past can hinder personal growth and prevent you from fully experiencing the present. It may lead to stagnation, resentment, or a constant longing for what it once was. While reflecting on past experiences can be valuable for learning and growth, it is essential to strike a balance and not let the past overshadow the present.

　　　On the other hand, living in the present involves fully engaging in the here and now, embracing the present moment with all its joys, challenges, and opportunities. It requires cultivating mindfulness, focusing on the current task or interaction, and being aware of one's thoughts, emotions, and surroundings. Living in the present enables you to appreciate the beauty of everyday moments, build stronger connections with others, and make the most of the opportunities that come your way.

Finding a balance between the past and the present is vital. Reflecting on the past can provide valuable lessons and insights while being present allows you to fully engage with life and make conscious choices that align with your values and goals. By practicing mindfulness, gratitude, and self-awareness, you can strive to live more in the present, savoring the richness of each moment and creating a fulfilling and meaningful life.

Question #53

Are you "clinging" to the future in hopes it will become better?

As you reflect on this question, it is an introspective exercise that allows you to examine your mindset and approach to life. Clinging to the future refers to focusing excessively on future outcomes or expectations, often believing they will bring greater happiness or fulfillment.

While goals and aspirations are essential, becoming too fixated on the future can prevent you from fully appreciating and engaging with the present moment. It can create a longing or dissatisfaction with the current circumstances, leading to feelings of restlessness or impatience.

It is essential to balance envisioning a better future and embracing the present moment. Rather than clinging to the future, you can practice mindfulness and gratitude to cultivate a deeper appreciation for the present and find contentment in the journey. This allows you to focus on your actions and choices today to create your desired future rather than placing all your happiness and fulfillment on a distant outcome.

By shifting your perspective and being fully present in each moment, you can find joy, growth, and meaning in the present while working towards a brighter future. Embracing the journey, being adaptable to change, and nurturing a positive mindset contribute to a more fulfilling and balanced approach to life. Letting go of excessive attachment to the future allows you to savor the present, make the most of opportunities, and live with greater peace and contentment.

Focusing on trusting the process is key. Trusting the process involves embracing the journey with faith and patience, recognizing that growth, learning, and transformation occur gradually. It encourages relinquishing undue fixation on immediate outcomes and surrendering to the rhythm of progression. Much like tending to a seed with patience, nurturing, and time, trusting the process invites us to believe in our efforts and allow the natural unfolding of events, knowing that each step contributes to the ultimate destination. It's a reminder that challenges and setbacks are integral parts of the journey, contributing to our resilience and eventual success.

Question #54

What aspects of the future appear more promising than your present circumstances?

      One aspect that may make the future seem better is the potential for personal growth and development. The future offers the possibility of learning new skills, gaining knowledge, and expanding your horizons. It promises new opportunities, experiences, and achievements that enrich your life and help you reach your full potential.

      Additionally, the future often represents a fresh start or a chance for change. It offers the potential to overcome challenges, break free from limitations, and embrace new beginnings. The future holds the promise of improved circumstances, whether it be in relationships, careers, health, or personal well-being. It is a blank canvas where you can envision a life that aligns more closely with your values, passions, and aspirations.

      Moreover, the future may offer a sense of hope and optimism. It provides the belief that with time and effort, things can get better. It is a reminder that challenges and difficulties faced in the present are not permanent, and there is potential for positive transformation. This belief in a brighter future can be a source of motivation, resilience, and perseverance as you work towards creating the desired reality.

While looking to the future with optimism and hope is natural, finding a balance and not solely focusing on what may be better is essential. Finding joy, contentment, and gratitude in the present is crucial while actively working toward the future we envision. By cultivating a healthy balance between embracing the present and working toward the future, we can live with a sense of purpose, fulfillment, and continuous growth.

The question "what aspects of the future appear more promising than your present circumstances?" prompts contemplation on the potential shifts and improvements one envisions in their life journey. It encourages individuals to look beyond their current reality and consider the horizon of possibilities that lie ahead. This question recognizes the human tendency to seek growth and progress, sparking a thoughtful examination of the aspirations and dreams that drive our actions.

As we ponder the question, we are invited to explore the areas where our present circumstances might fall short of our hopes and expectations. It provides an opportunity to identify specific areas for growth, whether they are related to personal development, career advancement, relationships, or other life dimensions. By acknowledging these disparities, we can begin to build a roadmap for the changes we wish to make in order to bridge the gap between our current reality and our envisioned future.

In essence, this question fuels a forward-looking perspective that balances aspiration with grounded self-awareness. It acknowledges that the path to a more promising future is not solely about escaping the present, but about aligning our choices, efforts, and intentions in a way that propels us toward a reality that resonates more authentically with our desires. Through introspection prompted by this question, we can lay the foundation for setting meaningful goals, cultivating resilience, and manifesting the changes that will ultimately lead us toward a future brimming with promise and potential.

Question #55

What can you do to start "bettering" life right now?

Considering what you can do to start "bettering" life right now is a powerful inquiry that empowers you to take immediate action toward personal growth and well-being. There are several steps you can take to start making positive changes and enhancing your overall quality of life.

First, cultivating self-awareness is essential. Taking time to reflect on your thoughts, emotions, and behaviors allows you to identify areas for improvement and recognize patterns that may be holding you back. In addition, by becoming more self-aware, you can gain insights into your strengths, weaknesses, values, and goals, which serve as a solid foundation for personal growth.

Second, setting meaningful goals is crucial. Establishing clear and achievable goals provides direction and purpose in life. Whether short-term or long-term goals, having a roadmap helps you stay focused and motivated; ensuring these goals align with your values and aspirations is essential, allowing you to channel your energy and efforts into endeavors that genuinely matter to me.

Additionally, taking small, consistent actions is vital to creating a "bettering" life. It can be as simple as incorporating healthy habits into your daily routine, such as exercising regularly, practicing mindfulness, or engaging in self-reflection. When done consistently, these small actions accumulate over time, leading to significant positive changes in various areas of life.

Moreover, seeking support and surrounding yourself with positive influences can significantly improve life. Whether connecting with a mentor, joining a supportive community, or seeking professional guidance, having a solid support system provides encouragement, accountability, and valuable insights. In addition, collaborating with others who share similar goals and values creates a supportive environment for personal growth and fosters a sense of belonging.

Taking steps to " better" life now requires self-awareness, goal-setting, consistent action, and a supportive network. By implementing these strategies, you can actively embark on a journey of personal growth and create a more fulfilling and meaningful life. Through continuous effort and commitment, you can make positive changes and embrace a life that aligns with your values and aspirations.

Question #56

Are you able to wake up and feel bliss with your current life?

Reflecting on your current life is an invitation to evaluate your happiness, contentment, and fulfillment. Feeling bliss is a deeply personal and subjective experience influenced by various factors, including one's mindset, circumstances, and outlook.

While it may be unrealistic to expect constant bliss in every moment, there is value in assessing the overall satisfaction and joy that you derive from your daily life. It involves considering whether you are living in alignment with your values, pursuing meaningful goals, and cultivating gratitude for the present moment.

If you are not waking up and feeling bliss with your current life, it may indicate areas that require attention and growth. For example, it could signify that you must reassess your priorities, adjust your lifestyle, or explore new passions and interests. It may also prompt you/one to examine any limiting beliefs or negative thought patterns obstructing your/one's ability to experience joy and contentment.

Moreover, finding bliss in life often involves actively nurturing positive habits and a mindset. This includes practicing self-care, nurturing relationships, engaging in activities that bring you joy, and practicing gratitude and mindfulness. It may also involve letting go of expectations, embracing imperfections, and being present at the moment.

Finding bliss in life is a journey that requires self-reflection, self-awareness, and intentional choices. It is about creating a life that aligns with your values and brings you joy and contentment. By consciously nurturing your well-being and pursuing what truly matters to you, you can increase the likelihood of waking up and feeling a sense of bliss with your current life.

Question #57

What defines happiness for you?

  Reflecting on what defines happiness is a deeply personal and introspective exploration. Happiness is a subjective feeling that varies from person to person, and it is crucial to express it in a way that resonates with your values, aspirations, and unique perspective on life.

  Happiness may not solely depend on external circumstances or material possessions. It goes beyond fleeting moments of pleasure and encompasses a more profound sense of well-being and fulfillment. It is about cultivating a positive mindset, embracing meaningful connections with others, and aligning with your values.

  Organic relationships and a sense of belonging are crucial elements of your happiness. Meaningful connections with family, friends, and a community that uplifts and supports you bring a deep understanding of joy and fulfillment. Sharing moments of love, compassion, and support with others nourishes your soul and contributes to your overall happiness.

Moreover, personal growth and self-fulfillment are critical components of your happiness. The pursuit of knowledge, self-improvement, and the ability to express your creativity and passions bring a sense of purpose and fulfillment. Being able to make a positive impact on the lives of others and contribute to something greater than yourself also brings immense happiness.

Your happiness may be holistic and a multifaceted experience that encompasses physical, emotional, and spiritual well-being. It involves balancing personal fulfillment, meaningful relationships, and a sense of purpose in life. By aligning your actions and choices with what brings you genuine joy and satisfaction, you can create a life that is true to yourself and embodies your definition of happiness.

This question delves into the very essence of personal fulfillment and contentment. It compels introspection, encouraging individuals to unravel the intricate tapestry of their emotions, values, and aspirations. This question recognizes the inherent subjectivity of happiness, acknowledging that its definition varies greatly from person to person. As we contemplate our unique sources of joy and the qualities that contribute to our sense of well-being, we are prompted to connect with our innermost selves and uncover the elements that bring meaning and purpose to our lives.

Question #58

What moment in your life did you feel the happiest?

      This question opens a window to cherished memories that illuminate the landscape of our personal joy. It encourages a nostalgic journey through our life's tapestry, highlighting a singular instance when our hearts danced with an unparalleled sense of elation. This inquiry not only invites us to revisit moments of profound happiness but also compels us to reflect on the factors that contributed to that felicity, deepening our understanding of the experiences, relationships, and aspirations that can shape our lasting well-being.

      This question is a nostalgic, reflective journey that may bring forth cherished memories and emotions. There are several instances in your life where you may have experienced profound happiness, making it challenging to pinpoint a defining moment. However, one memory that may stand out is when you achieved a personal goal you had been working towards for an extended period.

It shows a culmination of hard work, perseverance, and overcoming obstacles, leading to a profound sense of accomplishment and joy. The moment is filled with positive emotions—pride, satisfaction, and a deep understanding of fulfillment. It represents the culmination of your efforts and serves as a reminder of the power of determination and resilience.

What makes this moment particularly special is the achievement and the journey leading up to it. It is a testament to your personal and professional growth and reaffirms your belief in the power of setting goals and pursuing them with unwavering dedication.

Looking back, you may realize that true happiness often lies in pursuing meaningful goals and the process of personal growth. It is not solely about reaching the destination but rather the joy derived from the journey. This realization inspired you to embrace new challenges, set ambitious goals, and savor moments of growth and progress.

While these moments may stand out as a pinnacle of happiness, you will recognize that joy is not confined to a single event. Instead, it is a continuous journey comprising a collection of big and small moments that bring joy, gratitude, and a profound appreciation for life's blessings.

Question #59

What moment in your life did you feel the saddest?

This question leads us to explore the contours of our emotional landscape, delving into the depths of sorrow that have left their mark. It beckons us to revisit a time when the weight of sadness was most palpable, prompting introspection into the circumstances and emotions that enveloped us. This query not only allows us to acknowledge our vulnerabilities but also encourages a compassionate reflection on our capacity to endure and heal. As we recollect and contemplate our lowest points, we gain insights into our resilience, the strength that emerged from adversity, and the lessons that accompany even the most trying times.

There may have been moments of profound sadness in your life, making it challenging to single out just one as the saddest. However, one memory that may stand out is when/if you experienced losing a loved one.

The pain and grief accompanying this loss is overwhelming, and it may feel like your world has been shattered. It is a time of deep sorrow, confusion, and emptiness. Sadness is felt in every aspect of your life, and it seems like happiness will never return.

During this period of intense sadness, you learn the importance of embracing grief as a natural part of the human experience. It allows you to process your emotions, seek support from loved ones, and find solace in memories and cherished moments shared with the person you lost. It also teaches you the value of empathy and compassion as you witness the impact of loss not just on yourself but also on others.

While that moment remains imprinted in your memory as a time of profound sadness, it also serves as an incentive for personal growth and resilience. It reinforces the fragility of life and the need to cherish and appreciate every moment. It teaches you the importance of finding strength and seeking support when needed.

In retrospect, you may recognize that sadness is an inevitable part of the human experience and can provide valuable lessons and opportunities for growth. We can develop a deeper understanding of ourselves and the world by embracing and navigating moments of sadness. It reminds us to treasure moments of joy, improve resilience, and extend kindness and empathy to others experiencing their moments of sadness.

Question #60

What have you learned from loss?

  Loss is an inevitable part of life, and while it is undoubtedly painful, it also offers valuable insights and opportunities for growth.

  One of the most important lessons you may have learned from loss is the importance of cherishing and appreciating the people and experiences in your life. It serves as a reminder of the transient nature of life and the need to make the most of every moment. In addition, loss teaches you to cultivate gratitude for your relationships and connections, express love and appreciation openly, and prioritize meaningful connections over trivial matters.

  Loss may have also taught you the resilience of the human spirit. It reveals our capacity to endure pain, adapt to new circumstances, and find strength within ourselves. Through grieving, you learn that healing is not linear and takes time and self-compassion. It will show you the power of self-reflection and introspection, allowing you to navigate the complex emotions that arise and grow from the experience.

A loss will deepen your empathy and compassion towards others experiencing their grief and loss. It will heighten your awareness of people's struggles and the need for support and understanding during difficult times. Finally, it will inspire you to be more present for others, to lend a listening ear, and to offer a helping hand when needed.

Loss is a profound teacher that imparts invaluable wisdom. It reminds you to live with gratitude, embrace resilience, and extend compassion to others. It teaches you to treasure the moments and relationships in your life and to approach challenges with stability and strength. Ultimately, it underscores the fragility and preciousness of life, prompting you to make the most of each day and cherish the connections that bring joy and meaning to your existence.

This question directs our attention to a profound wellspring of growth hidden within the painful corridors of life. It compels us to reflect on the intricacies of grief, urging us to discern the lessons that emerge from the emptiness left behind by loss. Through this exploration, we come to recognize the impermanence of existence and the fragility of the human experience. Loss, in its myriad forms, becomes a teacher that imparts wisdom about the transient nature of life's treasures, urging us to cherish every moment and embrace the people and experiences that enrich our journey.

Furthermore, this question unravels the intricate tapestry of resilience, empathy, and personal transformation woven by the threads of loss. It illuminates the human capacity to navigate the abyss of sorrow and emerge with newfound strength. From loss, we learn the art of adaptation, of redefining our identities in the wake of change, and of summoning the courage to rebuild from the ruins. Loss is a crucible through which we forge empathy, for as we taste the bitterness of grief, we become more attuned to the pain of others. It teaches us to support, console, and stand alongside those whose hearts are heavy with their own losses. Ultimately, the lessons drawn from loss transcend the ache, guiding us towards a profound understanding of the human experience and fostering a deeper appreciation for the intricacies of life's journey.

Question #61

What is something you gave up that you wish you hadn't?

This question suggests moments of regret and contemplation. There may have been instances in your life where you made choices or let go of specific opportunities or relationships that, in hindsight, you deeply regret. However, as you reflect, one decision will stand out, reminding you of the importance of listening to your intuition and not succumbing to fear or external pressures.

There may have been a time when you had the chance to pursue a passion project or embark on a new adventure, but you let self-doubt and fear of failure hold you back. Looking back, you may have wished you had leaped, embraced the unknown, and followed your heart. The fear of regret often outweighs the fear of failure, and you may deeply regret not seizing that opportunity.

This reflection will teach you the significance of embracing courage and being open to taking risks. It serves as a reminder to trust your instincts, embrace uncertainty, and live without regrets. Finally, it is a valuable lesson that encourages you to make choices aligned with your passions and values, even if they involve stepping out of your comfort zone.

This question delves into the realm of reflection and regret, prompting us to confront the intersections of choice and consequence in our lives. It beckons us to peer into the past and contemplate the paths not taken, the decisions that led to relinquishing something meaningful. This query resonates with the universal human experience of grappling with the bittersweet realization that certain choices resulted in parting ways with aspirations, relationships, or opportunities that once held deep significance.

In pondering this question, we confront the complexities of hindsight, acknowledging that our choices are often made with the best intentions based on the knowledge and circumstances at hand. Yet, it also highlights the intricate interplay between growth and sacrifice, urging us to recognize that even in relinquishing something dear, there can be hidden gems of wisdom, resilience, and transformation. This introspection can inspire a renewed appreciation for the present and a mindfulness about the choices we make moving forward, emphasizing the importance of aligning our actions with our deepest aspirations to avoid future sentiments of longing and unfulfilled potential.

Moving forward, may you stay committed to honoring your dreams and desires. May you strive to make choices that align with your authentic self. May you resist the urge to let fear or self-doubt dictate your decisions, and, instead, you will embrace the unknown with a sense of curiosity and determination. This reflection will ignite a renewed sense of purpose and remind you of the importance of pursuing what truly matters to you without regret or hesitation.

Question #62

What is the meaning of your life?

Contemplating the meaning of life is a profoundly philosophical and introspective inquiry that has puzzled humanity for centuries. While there is no definitive answer, everyone's interpretation of life's meaning is unique and deeply personal. For most, the meaning of life lies in the pursuit of purpose, personal growth, and meaningful connections.

Life gains significance through the pursuit of one's passions and the realization of one's potential. It is about discovering and embracing our unique talents and using them to impact the world positively. The meaning of life is intricately woven into the journey of self-discovery as we uncover our values, passions, and the things that bring us joy and fulfillment.

The question embarks on a profound journey into the heart of existential contemplation, inviting us to explore the purpose and significance that underpin our existence. This question encapsulates the age-old quest to uncover the essence of our being, intertwining philosophy, spirituality, and personal introspection. As we reflect on this question, we grapple with the intricate tapestry of identity, purpose, and the pursuit of fulfillment.

This prompts us to navigate the diverse landscapes of our experiences, values, and aspirations. It acknowledges the uncertainty and evolution of meaning, recognizing that the answers might transform over time in response to life's evolving circumstances. While there may not be a single definitive answer, exploring the question "What is the meaning of your life?" sparks a process of self-discovery, encouraging us to seek alignment between our innermost desires and the impact we wish to have on the world. Ultimately, this question serves as a compass, guiding us toward a purposeful and fulfilling existence as we navigate the complexities of our human journey.

The meaning of life is a deeply personal and subjective quest. It is about finding what brings us joy, purpose, and fulfillment and aligning our actions and values with those discoveries. It is about embracing the present moment, living authentically, and leaving a positive legacy. The meaning of life may evolve and change as we grow and learn, but pursuing personal growth, meaningful connections, and life aligned with our passions and values gives life its intrinsic meaning.

Question #63

What motivates you?

Motivation is a driving force behind human actions, decisions, and goals. People are motivated by a variety of factors, including:

1. *Personal Fulfillment*: Many individuals are motivated by the desire to achieve personal growth, self-improvement, and a sense of accomplishment. This can include pursuing hobbies, learning new skills, or completing challenges.

2. *External Recognition*: Some people are motivated by external validation, such as praise, awards, or recognition from others. This recognition can reinforce their sense of worth and drive them to excel.

3. *Financial Incentives*: Money and financial security are powerful motivators for many people. The need to provide for oneself and

one's family can drive individuals to work hard and pursue higher-paying opportunities.

4. *Passion and Interest*: When individuals are passionate about a particular subject or activity, they are often naturally motivated to engage in it. Passion can fuel sustained effort and dedication.

5. *Social Connection*: The desire for social interaction and belonging can be a strong motivator. People may engage in activities to build and maintain relationships, both in personal and professional spheres.

6. *Impact and Contribution*: Making a positive impact on the world or contributing to a greater cause can be highly motivating. This can include activities related to volunteering, charity work, or advocacy.

7. *Personal Values*: Individuals are often motivated by aligning their actions with their deeply held values and beliefs. Acting in accordance with one's principles can provide a sense of purpose.

8. *Competition*: Some people are motivated by competition and the desire to outperform others. The challenge of overcoming obstacles and surpassing benchmarks can drive them forward.

9. *Fear and Survival*: Survival instincts can also be motivating factors. The need to avoid danger, meet basic needs, and ensure personal safety can drive action.

It's important to note that motivation can be complex and multifaceted, and different people are motivated by different combinations of these factors. Additionally, motivations can change over time based on life circumstances, experiences, and personal development.

If you're seeking to understand your own motivations, introspection and self-awareness are valuable tools. Reflecting on your goals, values, interests, and emotional responses can help you gain insight into what drives you to take action and make choices.

Question #64

Who are the five people you spend the most time with?

Contemplating the question of the five people you spend the most time with highlights the significant influence our social circle has on our lives. The individuals we surround ourselves with can shape our mindsets, beliefs, and aspirations. Therefore, evaluating the composition of your inner circle helps you gain insights into the dynamics of your relationships and their impact on your personal growth.

This question touches on the idea that the individuals we interact with on a regular basis can significantly influence our thoughts, behaviors, and overall outlook on life. This concept is often attributed to motivational speaker Jim Rohn, who suggested that we become the average of the five people we spend the most time with.

The following factors contribute to our social circles:

1. *Influence and Impact:* The people we surround ourselves with have a profound impact on our lives. Their attitudes, beliefs, and behaviors can shape our own perspectives and choices. It's important to consider whether these influences are positive and aligned with our personal goals.

2. *Diverse Relationships*: Reflecting on the five people we spend the most time with can reveal the diversity of our relationships. These individuals might include family members, friends, colleagues, mentors, or romantic partners. Each relationship contributes a unique set of experiences and perspectives to our lives.

3. *Support and Growth*: Close relationships can provide emotional support and contribute to personal growth. When we're surrounded by individuals who encourage us, challenge us, and believe in our potential, we're more likely to strive for success and navigate challenges effectively.

4. *Shared Values*: The people we choose to spend time with often share similar values, interests, and goals. This shared foundation can create a sense of belonging and strengthen our sense of identity.

5. *Evaluation and Adjustment*: Reflecting on the individuals we're most connected to can prompt us to evaluate whether these relationships are beneficial or if they might be holding us back. Sometimes, we need to make intentional choices to distance ourselves from negative influences and seek out positive ones.

6. *Networking and Opportunities*: The people in our circles can open doors to various opportunities, both personally and professionally. Networking and connections can lead to collaborations, partnerships, and introductions that can be valuable for our growth.

7. *Reciprocity and Give-and-Take*: Healthy relationships are built on a balance of give-and-take. Reflecting on who we spend time with can remind us to contribute positively to these relationships and ensure that our interactions are mutually beneficial.

8. *Impact on Self-Perception:* The way others perceive us can influence our self-esteem and self-image. Positive relationships can contribute to a strong sense of self-worth, while negative relationships can erode our confidence.

9. *Intentional Choices:* Ultimately, we have a degree of control over the people we choose to spend time with. Reflecting on this question can encourage us to be intentional about nurturing relationships that align with our personal and professional aspirations.

In a world where social interactions can occur both in-person and online, it's important to consider the digital connections we engage with as well. Social media, online forums, and virtual communities also contribute to the circle of people who influence us, even if we don't physically spend time with them.

Remember that the quality of our relationships matters more than the quantity. Building and maintaining positive, meaningful connections can have a significant impact on our overall well-being and success.

Question #65

Do these five people bring out the best in you? If not, is it time to let them go?

Surrounding yourself with individuals who uplift, inspire, and encourage personal growth is crucial for your overall well-being and success.

Ideally, the people you spend the most time with should be sources of positivity, support, and motivation. They should believe in your abilities, challenge you to reach new heights, and provide a nurturing environment for personal development. When these qualities are present in your relationships, they create a synergistic effect that fosters mutual growth and fulfillment.

However, if specific individuals in your social circle consistently bring negativity, undermine your confidence, or discourage your aspirations, it may be time to reassess those connections. Toxic relationships can drain your energy, hinder your progress, and impede your journey toward self-improvement. Recognizing the detrimental impact of such relationships is a vital step towards prioritizing your well-being and personal growth.

While letting go of relationships can be difficult, it is crucial to surround yourself with individuals who align with your values, goals, and aspirations. Choosing to distance yourself from those who hinder your growth is not a selfish act but rather an act of self-care and self-preservation. Furthermore, it opens space for positive influences and allows you to cultivate relationships that inspire, challenge, and bring out your best.

Evaluating the impact of the five people you spend the most time with reminds you to be intentional about the company you keep. By fostering relationships with individuals who genuinely support your growth and bring out the best in you, it creates an environment that nurtures your potential, encourages your aspirations, and enables you to become the best version of yourself.

Question #66

Are you afraid of letting others in? Why?

This question reveals the complex dynamics of trust, vulnerability, and self-preservation. It is natural to experience some hesitancy or fear when opening up to others, as it involves a certain level of emotional risk. However, understanding the reasons behind this fear can help shed light on the underlying factors holding you back.

One possible reason for hesitancy is a fear of rejection or judgment. The vulnerability that comes with letting others in means exposing your true thoughts, emotions, and experiences, making you feel exposed and susceptible to criticism or rejection. This fear can stem from past experiences of hurt or betrayal, causing you to build walls and guard yourself against potential pain.

Another factor contributing to the fear of letting others in could be the fear of being vulnerable and losing control. Sharing personal experiences and emotions requires a certain level of surrender, which can feel unsettling. In addition, it involves allowing others to see you in your raw and authentic state, which can be uncomfortable and uncertain.

Additionally, the fear of letting others in may stem from a fear of dependency or losing one's sense of individuality. Opening up to others can create a sense of reliance and interdependence, which can be perceived as a loss of autonomy. The fear of losing oneself or becoming overly dependent on others can lead to a reluctance to let others in.

Understanding these underlying fears and hesitations is the first step toward addressing them. Recognizing that vulnerability and trust are essential for building meaningful connections and fostering personal growth is important. By gradually opening up and building trust with individuals who demonstrate empathy, understanding, and support, you can overcome these fears and create more profound and fulfilling relationships. Through vulnerability, genuine connections are formed, and the rewards of authentic connections often outweigh the temporary discomfort of letting others in.

Question #67

What kind of people do you enjoy spending time with?

Contemplating the kind of people you enjoy spending time with reveals the qualities and characteristics that resonate with you on a deeper level. These individuals could contribute to your overall well-being and enrich your life meaningfully.

You may find yourself gravitating toward people who possess genuine authenticity. Being themselves, without deception or masks, creates an environment of trust and openness. If so, you may value individuals who are comfortable in their skin and embrace their uniqueness, as it encourages you to do the same.

You may also enjoy spending time with optimistic people. Their positive energy is contagious, uplifting your spirits and helping you to maintain a positive mindset. Being around individuals who see the silver lining in situations and approach challenges with a can-do attitude fosters an environment of growth and inspiration.

Furthermore, you may be drawn to individuals who are intellectually stimulating and have a thirst for knowledge. Engaging in thought-provoking conversations and sharing ideas with curious minds ignites your intellectual curiosity and expands your perspective. Finally, you may appreciate individuals who challenge you intellectually, pushing you to explore new ideas and question your beliefs.

Lastly, you may find great joy in the company of compassionate and empathetic individuals. Their ability to understand and connect with others on an emotional level fosters deep and meaningful connections. These individuals listen attentively, offer support without judgment, and display genuine care for the well-being of others.

The people you should enjoy spending time with should be authentic, positive, intellectually stimulating, and compassionate. They will uplift, inspire, and challenge you, fostering an environment of growth, connection, and personal fulfillment. Surrounding yourself with individuals who embody these qualities enriches your life and contributes to your overall well-being and happiness.

Question #68

How can you be the type of person you described in your response to Question #67?

       Becoming the type of person you described in your previous response involves a conscious commitment to personal growth and self-improvement. While it may require effort and dedication, there are several steps you can take to embody the qualities you search for in others.

       First and foremost, fostering self-awareness is essential. Understanding your strengths and areas for growth allows you to actively work on developing the qualities you desire. This involves reflecting on your thoughts, actions, and interactions with others and consciously aligning them with your ideals.

       Practicing authenticity is another crucial aspect. By being true to yourself and embracing your uniqueness, you can create an environment where others feel comfortable doing the same. This involves embracing vulnerability, letting go of the need for approval, and expressing yourself honestly and authentically in all aspects of life.

       Promoting positivity and optimism requires shifting your mindset. This can be achieved through gratitude, mindfulness, and reframing negative thoughts. In addition, you can develop a more optimistic mindset by consciously focusing on the positive aspects of situations, maintaining a hopeful attitude, and surrounding yourself with positive influences.

Lastly, developing empathy and compassion involves actively understanding others' perspectives and experiences. This includes practicing active listening, being non-judgmental, and showing genuine care and concern for others' well-being. Regularly engaging in acts of kindness and compassion can also help foster these qualities.

Ultimately, embodying the qualities you admire in others is an ongoing process that requires self-reflection, a conscious effort, and a commitment to personal growth. By continuously striving to be the best version of yourself, you can cultivate the qualities of authenticity, positivity, intellectual curiosity, and compassion that you value and, in turn, inspire and positively impact those around you.

Question #69

Which is worse – never trying or fear of failing?

While both options have their consequences, the implications of each can vary greatly depending on individual perspectives and circumstances.

Never trying can be seen as a missed opportunity for growth, learning, and self-discovery. On the other hand, it represents a reluctance to step out of one's comfort zone and take a chance at something meaningful. By never trying, we limit our potential and deny ourselves the possibility of achieving our goals and dreams. The fear of failure may hold us back, but the regret of not trying can haunt us indefinitely.

Not trying or the fear of failing can be viewed as a stagnant existence devoid of growth and progress. Although often perceived negatively, failure is a vital part of the learning process. It provides valuable lessons, resilience, and the opportunity to adapt and improve. By never experiencing failure, we may shield ourselves from essential life lessons and the chance to develop new skills or perspectives.

Ultimately, the fear of failure often drives the notion that never trying is worse. However, by embracing failure as a natural part of the journey and reframing it as an opportunity for growth, we can overcome the paralysis of inaction. Taking calculated risks, pursuing our passions, and stepping outside our comfort zones can lead to personal growth, self-discovery, and the fulfillment that comes from knowing we gave it our all.

While the fear of failure may be daunting, the regret of never trying can be equally detrimental. Therefore, balancing calculated risks and embracing failure as a stepping-stone to success is vital. By acknowledging that failure is a necessary part of the journey and approaching it with resilience and a growth mindset, we can navigate the challenges and uncertainties of life with courage and determination.

Question #70

Are you more of a leader or follower?

Reflecting on whether you are more of a leader or follower requires introspection into your natural inclinations, strengths, and preferences when taking charge or following the lead of others. While there is value in both leadership and being a follower, understanding where you thrive and contribute the most is essential for personal growth and effective collaboration.

In certain situations, you may find yourself naturally drawn to leadership roles. For example, you may enjoy taking the initiative, setting goals, and guiding others toward a shared vision. Leadership allows you to utilize your strengths in decision-making, problem-solving, and inspiring others. It provides an opportunity to shape outcomes, influence change, and positively impact a team or organization. Leadership also provides a platform for personal growth and the development of leadership skills that can be valuable in various aspects of life.

However, there are times when you might be more comfortable as a follower. For example, you may recognize the importance of being part of a team, contributing your skills and expertise to support a collective effort. As a follower, you are receptive to the ideas and guidance of others, demonstrating adaptability and the ability to work collaboratively towards a shared goal. Followership allows you to learn from others, build relationships, and contribute to the success of a larger vision without the burden of sole responsibility.

The distinction between being a leader or follower is flexible. It is a dynamic continuum where one's role may vary depending on the context, the individuals involved, and the specific goals or objectives. Recognizing your strengths, adapting to different positions, and embracing opportunities to lead or follow enable you to navigate diverse situations effectively and contribute meaningfully to personal and collective growth.

Question #71

Do you believe in the Law of Attraction?

This question refers to the concept that thoughts and intentions can influence our reality and attract specific outcomes into our lives. This idea suggests that positive or negative thoughts and energies can shape our experiences. The law of attraction, recently, has gained popularity through various books, teachings, and self-help practices.

Here are a few reflections on this question and the concept of the law of attraction:

1. *Subjective Beliefs*: Belief in the law of attraction is a subjective matter. Some people strongly believe in its principles and have experienced what they perceive as evidence of its effects in their lives. Others are more skeptical and view the concept as pseudoscience or wishful thinking.

2. *Mindset and Positivity*: One key aspect of the law of attraction is the emphasis on maintaining a positive mindset. Regardless of whether one believes in the metaphysical aspects of attraction, adopting a positive attitude can have tangible psychological benefits, including reduced stress and improved overall well-being.

3. *Visualization and Goal Setting*: The practice of visualizing desired outcomes and setting clear goals is often associated with the law of attraction. Visualization can help individuals clarify their objectives and stay focused on what they want to achieve.

4. *Focus and Action*: A common criticism of the law of attraction is that it might lead some individuals to believe that merely thinking positively will automatically bring about their desired outcomes. However, many proponents of the concept emphasize that positive thinking must be accompanied by focused action and effort to achieve results.

5. *Confirmation Bias*: Those who believe in the law of attraction might be more likely to notice instances where their positive thoughts seem to align with positive outcomes, reinforcing their belief. This is known as confirmation bias, where people tend to seek out and remember information that supports their existing beliefs.

6. *Scientific Validity*: The law of attraction doesn't align with established scientific principles, such as the laws of physics and causality. As a result, it's often criticized by skeptics who argue that there's no empirical evidence to support its claims.

7. *Psychological Aspects*: Regardless of the metaphysical aspects, the law of attraction draws attention to the psychological impact of our thoughts and beliefs. Positive thinking can boost confidence, resilience, and overall motivation, which can contribute to achieving one's goals.

8. *Personal Empowerment*: Believers in the law of attraction often find a sense of empowerment in the idea that they have some control over their circumstances through their thoughts and intentions.

9. *Individual Experiences*: People's experiences with the law of attraction can vary widely. Some may attribute positive changes to their conscious efforts, while others may view these changes as coincidences or the natural outcomes of their actions.

In the end, whether one believes in the law of attraction or not is a personal choice. Some individuals find value in its principles as a guiding philosophy, while others approach life with different perspectives. It's important to critically evaluate any concept and determine what resonates with your own beliefs and experiences.

Question #72

Does commitment scare you? If so, why?

Reflecting on whether commitment scares you requires a deeper exploration of your personal experiences, beliefs, and fears. While commitment can bring stability, growth, and deeper connections, it can also evoke uncertainty and vulnerability. It could stagnate your growth since commitment could lead to comfort and comfort kills growth.

Commitment involves making a firm decision and dedicating oneself to a particular action or relationship. It often requires long-term dedication, responsibility, and the willingness to invest time, effort, and emotions. Commitment also implies a level of vulnerability and the potential for emotional investment. Opening oneself to commitment means exposing vulnerabilities and entrusting others with our deepest desires and needs.

This vulnerability can be intimidating, as it tells us of the risk of rejection, heartbreak, or disappointment. The fear of getting hurt or being let down may deter us from fully embracing commitment. The fear of commitment may stem from various factors, such as past experiences of disappointment or betrayal, fear of the unknown, or a desire to maintain freedom and avoid feeling trapped or restricted.

However, it is crucial to recognize that commitment can also bring immense rewards. It allows for deeper connections, personal growth, and the opportunity to build a meaningful and fulfilling life. Recognizing that commitment can also yield substantial rewards is essential, as it paves the way for profound connections, catalyzes personal growth, and opens avenues for constructing a life that is both rich in meaning and fulfillment. Embracing commitment fosters the cultivation of lasting relationships, while the dedication to a purpose or goal serves as a crucible for self-improvement. Through steadfast commitment, the tapestry of life is woven with threads of purpose, resilience, and the joy of nurturing bonds that enrich our journey.

Overcoming the fear of commitment involves self-reflection, understanding one's worries and beliefs, and building trust in oneself and others. It requires taking small steps towards commitment and allowing oneself to experience the rewards and growth that can come from embracing responsibility in various aspects of life.

While commitment may evoke fear and uncertainty, it is essential to recognize its potential for personal growth and fulfillment. By exploring the underlying reasons for our fear of commitment and gradually building trust, we can overcome these fears and open ourselves up to the possibilities and rewards that come with genuine commitment. Embracing commitment requires courage, vulnerability, and a willingness to step outside our comfort zones, but it can lead to deeper connections, personal growth, and a more prosperous, more fulfilling life.

Question #73

Do any of the things you used to care about still impact your life?

As you read this question, you may feel a sense of nostalgia and introspection. It prompts you to revisit your past interests, priorities, and values and evaluate their evolution. While some of the things you used to care about may still hold significance, others may have diminished in importance or been replaced by new interests and concerns.

The impact of these past concerns on your present self varies. Some of them may still resonate with you, evoking emotions of familiarity and nostalgia. They may bring joy, inspiration, or a reminder of the values and aspirations shaping your journey. Realizing that some aspects of your past positively influence your present life could be reassuring, serving as a foundation for personal growth and fulfillment.

However, there may also be instances where the things you used to care about no longer hold the same weight or relevance. As time progresses, our interests, priorities, and values naturally evolve. Letting go of attachments to outdated concerns could be liberating, allowing space for new experiences, perspectives, and growth. It may initially evoke feelings of loss or disconnect, but ultimately, it could pave the way for personal transformation and exploring new passions and interests.

The realization that some of the things you used to care about still affect you highlights the dynamic nature of personal growth. It reminds you to embrace change, continuously reassess your values and priorities, and remain open to new experiences. It is a testament to the uncertainty of life and the potential for ongoing evolution and self-discovery. By acknowledging the impact of the past and embracing the present, you can navigate a path of personal fulfillment and find resonance in the things that truly matter to you now.

Question #74

What do you wish you would have done more?

    Reflecting on this question may prompt you to examine the choices and opportunities you have encountered along your journey and consider the paths *not* taken. While it is natural to have moments of longing or regret, it is essential to approach this reflection with compassion and a growth-oriented mindset.

    Frequently, we find ourselves wishing we had done more things like taking risks and stepping outside of our comfort zone. Life presents countless opportunities for growth, learning, and new experiences, but sometimes fear or hesitation holds us back. Looking back, we may recognize instances where we played it safe and opted for familiarity rather than embracing the unknown. These moments serve as reminders to seize the opportunities that arise, even with uncertainty or the possibility of failure.

    Additionally, we may wish we had invested more time and energy in nurturing meaningful connections and relationships. In the fast-paced nature of life, it can be easy to prioritize personal pursuits or become absorbed in day-to-day responsibilities. However, relationships are the foundation of our support systems, emotional well-being, and personal fulfillment. Fostering connections and investing in the people who matter most to you is something you may wish you had made a greater priority.

You may find yourself longing for more moments of presence and mindfulness. Life moves swiftly, and it is easy to get caught up in the hecticness of everyday routines. In doing so, we may miss the simple joys and beauty surrounding us. You may wish you had cultivated a greater awareness and appreciation for the present moment, savoring each experience and being fully present with the people and activities that bring you joy.

While reflecting on what you wish you would have done more of can bring a sense of longing or regret, it also serves as a reminder of the opportunities ahead. It prompts you to embrace the present moment, seize new experiences, nurture meaningful connections, and enrich a continuous growth and exploration mindset. Each day presents a chance to align your actions with these aspirations, ensuring you make the most of the journey ahead.

Looking back on missed opportunities or unfulfilled desires might stir feelings of regret, yet this introspection can also ignite a proactive spark for the future. It compels you to seize the current instant, embark on novel ventures, cultivate meaningful relationships, and foster an unceasing spirit of development and discovery. Every sunrise brings an occasion to harmonize your deeds with these ambitions, ensuring that the path ahead is traversed to its fullest potential.

Question #75

What's more important to you - doing the right thing or doing things right?

      This question reveals an interesting tension between ethics and execution. Of course, both aspects hold significance, but ultimately, doing the right thing takes precedence in one's value system.

      Doing the right thing encompasses moral and ethical considerations. It involves making choices that align with your principles, values, and the greater good. This means prioritizing integrity, honesty, compassion, and fairness in your actions and decisions. Doing the right thing extends beyond personal gain or immediate outcomes and considers the broader impact on individuals, communities, and the world. It involves a sense of responsibility and a commitment to act in ways that contribute positively to society.

      While doing things right involves precision, efficiency, and attention to detail, it becomes meaningful when it serves the purpose of doing the right thing. Striving for excellence, accuracy, and effectiveness in execution is essential, as it ensures that our actions have the desired impact and yield the best possible outcomes.

Striking a balance between the two is vital; doing the right thing embodies moral integrity and a sense of purpose, while doing things right emphasizes meticulous execution and achieving optimal outcomes. The synergy between ethical principles and effective execution ensures that our actions align with our values while maximizing the positive impact of our endeavors. Ultimately, the interplay between these aspects shapes our character and defines our contributions to the world.

Question #76

Do the books adorning your shelf or desk reflect a journey of ongoing exploration and growth, or do they patiently await the transformative touch of your engagement?

Given that you are currently reading this book, my assumption is that you are an avid reader. This question encourages a profound consideration of one's relationship with knowledge and personal development. It prompts us to assess whether the books in our physical space mirror our commitment to continuous learning and self-improvement, or if they represent untapped potential, waiting to be activated through our conscious engagement. This question underscores the dynamic interplay between intention and action in our pursuit of growth, urging us to recognize the significance of actively absorbing the wisdom and insights these books hold and to infuse our surroundings with the energy of curiosity and purposeful evolution.

This question also invites us to contemplate the symbolism behind the books we choose to keep within our immediate environment. Each book embodies the knowledge, experiences, and perspectives of its author, offering us a chance to embark on intellectual journeys that expand our horizons. When these books are left unopened, they embody untapped potential—potential that can catalyze shifts in our thinking, catalyze personal evolution, and enrich the tapestry of our lives. As we contemplate on these literary companions, we are prompted to consider the narrative of our own growth. Are we actively participating in the stories they offer, or do they remain frozen in time, capturing a momentary desire for growth that has yet to be actualized?

Ultimately, this question serves as a reminder that personal growth requires both intention and action. The books that decorate our space can be seen as allies on our journey, offering guidance, wisdom, and fresh perspectives. They beckon us to immerse ourselves in their pages, to challenge our assumptions, and to absorb insights that can propel us forward. As we answer this question, we are presented with a choice: to embrace these literary companions as catalysts for change or to let them remain silent witnesses to our inertia. In this reflection, we find an opportunity to infuse our lives with intentionality, to actively engage with the resources at our fingertips, and to embark on a continuous voyage of discovery and transformation.

Question #77

Do the thoughts that occupy your mind during the quiet hours of the night serve as allies in your journey of personal growth, or do they stand as barriers that hinder your progress?

This question prompts us to delve into the intimate landscape of our mind, especially when it's unguarded during the tranquil moments before sleep. It encourages us to evaluate the nature of our nocturnal contemplations—whether they're infused with positivity, hope, and aspirations that uplift our personal evolution, or whether they tend to be weighed down by worries, doubts, and self-limiting beliefs that impede our advancement.

Notably, the thoughts that occupy our mind just before sleep have a unique potency. As we transition into the realm of dreams, our subconscious mind is particularly receptive to the messages we feed it. This transition period offers a precious opportunity for these thoughts to linger and intermingle within us throughout the night. Like seeds planted in fertile soil, they have the potential to take root and influence our psyche, emotions, and even our actions during the waking hours.

Contemplating this question urges us to become conscious curators of our thought patterns, especially when the canvas of our mind is most receptive. It encourages us to cultivate a sense of mindfulness in our moments of vulnerability, ensuring that the thoughts we allow to take center stage as we drift into slumber contribute positively to our personal growth.

Amidst the stillness of the night, the question beckons us to become attuned to the essence of our inner dialogue. It nudges us to recognize that the thoughts we nurture as we close our eyes have a profound influence on our subconscious state. By confronting this question, we step into a realm of self-awareness where we acknowledge the potential of the night's silence to shape our mindset and, in turn, our personal journey. As we navigate the connection between our waking consciousness and the realm of dreams, we are empowered to shape a narrative that aligns with our aspirations and propels us forward along the path of growth.

Question #78

What is your personal sanctuary, and how does it nurture your well-being?

     Here, I invite you to explore the spaces, people, and activities that provide comfort, security, and a sense of refuge in your life. Having a sanctuary where you can retreat, recharge, and find solace amidst life's challenges and uncertainties is essential.

     Your safe place can manifest in different forms. It could be a physical location, such as a cozy corner in your home, a favorite park, or a serene natural setting. Being in these spaces should allow you to disconnect from the outside world and find peace and tranquility. These spaces could offer a breather from the demands of everyday life and provide an opportunity for self-reflection, relaxation, and rejuvenation.

     Your safe place can also exist within certain relationships or connections. It could be a trusted friend, a supportive family member, or a compassionate mentor who provides a safe and non-judgmental space for you to express your thoughts, feelings, and vulnerabilities. These individuals could offer comfort, understanding, and validation, helping you navigate life's ups and downs with greater resilience and emotional support.

Your safe place may also be found in activities or hobbies that bring you joy, fulfillment, and a sense of purpose. For example, engaging in creative pursuits, physical exercise, or mindfulness practices can be a haven from life's stresses. They allow you to fully immerse yourself in the present moment, fostering a sense of inner peace and providing a source of personal growth and self-expression.

Recognizing and nurturing your safe place is crucial for your overall well-being. It serves as an anchor during challenging times, offering stability, comfort, and a reminder of the available resources and support. By intentionally creating and embracing these safe spaces, relationships, and activities, you develop a sense of security, belonging, and resilience in your life journey.

Question #79

Where or with whom do you feel most comfortable?

    Focus on what is comfortable and highlight the importance of nurturing environments and relationships that encourage a sense of ease and authenticity. Comfort is a fundamental human need; finding spaces and individuals with whom you can be yourself is vital.

    Often, one could feel most comfortable in the sanctuary of their home. It may be a space that reflects your personality and values, providing a sense of familiarity, security, and peace. Within the walls of your home, you may relax, recharge, and freely express yourself without judgment or pretense. It may be a haven where you can surround yourself with the things and memories that bring you joy and create an environment that resonates with your innermost self.

    In terms of people, you may feel most comfortable with those who genuinely accept and support you for who you are. These individuals create a safe and nurturing space where you can be vulnerable, share your thoughts and emotions, and feel heard and understood. They provide a non-judgmental presence and offer unconditional love and support, allowing you to lower your guard and be yourself. Whether it's a close friend, a family member, or a partner, their presence brings a sense of warmth, connection, and emotional security.

Moreover, you may feel most comfortable in the presence of individuals who share similar values, interests, and perspectives. These connections create a sense of belonging and companionship, allowing for deeper relationships and mutual understanding. Engaging with like-minded individuals fosters a sense of comfort and validation, as we can relate to and support each other on our journeys.

Understanding where and with whom you feel most comfortable enables you to intentionally create and seek out these environments and relationships in your life. By surrounding yourself with supportive people and nurturing spaces, you can cultivate a sense of comfort and authenticity, allowing you to thrive and grow as your most authentic self.

Question #80

If you could eliminate one of your weaknesses, what would it be and why?

You may or may not recognize the inherent imperfections and areas of growth required within yourself. While weaknesses can provide opportunities for learning and development, it may be important to contemplate which one you would choose to eliminate if given a chance.

This question encapsulates the essence of self-awareness and personal growth. This inquiry prompts us to engage in profound introspection, inviting us to confront our vulnerabilities with courage and honesty. It acknowledges that we are all a tapestry of strengths and weaknesses, and that the journey towards self-improvement involves acknowledging and addressing these facets.

Identifying a weakness that we would choose to eliminate requires a deep dive into our inner landscape. It compels us to peel back the layers and reveal the areas where we feel limited or held back. In doing so, we come face to face with aspects of ourselves that might have been hidden from conscious awareness. This process is not about self-criticism, but about fostering a compassionate dialogue with ourselves, understanding that acknowledging our weaknesses is a step towards growth.

The question further encourages us to examine the reasons behind our choice. What drives us to eliminate a particular weakness? Is it hindering our progress, limiting our potential, or affecting our relationships? Delving into the "why" invites us to consider the impact our weaknesses have on various aspects of our lives. It urges us to connect the dots between our personal growth and our overarching goals, fostering a connection between our vulnerabilities and the transformation we seek.

Ultimately, the question serves as a catalyst for action. It propels us to move beyond theoretical self-reflection and towards practical steps for improvement. As we identify a weakness and understand its implications, we are better equipped to create strategies for growth. The process may involve seeking guidance, practicing new habits, or undergoing meaningful experiences that facilitate change. By addressing our weaknesses with intention and dedication, we set the stage for a journey of self-mastery, self-compassion, and enduring personal development.

Question #81

Do you hold grudges? Do you believe in forgiveness?

Reflecting on holding grudges versus believing in forgiveness prompts a deeper exploration of your beliefs and attitudes towards forgiveness and resentment.

May you believe in forgiveness and strive to embody it in your interactions with others. Holding grudges can be emotionally draining and hinder personal growth and healthy relationships. By embracing forgiveness, you release yourself from resentment and create space for healing and reconciliation.

Forgiveness is a transformative act that allows you let go of negative emotions, promotes empathy, and fosters compassion. It does not mean condoning or forgetting hurtful actions, but rather, it empowers you to move forward with greater peace and freedom. In addition, extending forgiveness cultivates understanding and empathy, promoting emotional well-being and fostering healthier connections with others, though not necessarily with the person you may be forgiving. Bear in mind, forgive but don't forget. By forgiving, we find solace, yet this doesn't imply that the forgiven person will necessarily retain a place in the forgiver's life.

Forgiveness is an essential component of personal growth and self-empowerment. It liberates you from bitterness and resentment, enabling you to focus on your growth and happiness rather than dwelling on past grievances. Forgiveness is a gift you give yourself, allowing you to break free from the cycle of negativity and embrace a more positive and fulfilling life.

However, it is essential to acknowledge that forgiveness is a deeply personal process, and it may take time and effort to cultivate. It does not mean that you should overlook or tolerate repeated harmful behavior, but rather, it involves setting healthy boundaries, seeking understanding, and working toward reconciliation when appropriate.

While holding grudges may seem tempting, natural, or even instinctive as a survival tool in moments of anger or hurt, forgiveness is a powerful tool for personal growth, emotional well-being, and healthy relationships. By embracing forgiveness, you can create a more peaceful and compassionate world within yourself and extend that compassion to others.

The act of forgiveness doesn't necessarily absolve the wrongdoer of their actions, nor does it mean that the hurt you experienced was insignificant. Instead, it acknowledges your own resilience and strength—the ability to rise above pain and find a path to healing.

Furthermore, holding onto grudges can become a burden that weighs you down, preventing you from fully embracing the present and moving forward. It can consume precious mental and emotional energy, leaving little room for positive experiences and personal development. When you choose forgiveness, you release yourself from the grip of past negativity, allowing space for growth, positivity, and new opportunities to enter your life.

Forgiveness isn't a one-size-fits-all process; it's a journey that unfolds differently for each person and situation. It may require time, reflection, and even moments of revisiting emotions that need healing. The key is to approach forgiveness with a compassionate heart, both towards yourself and the person who wronged you. By doing so, you create an environment of empathy and understanding, fostering emotional freedom and paving the way for a brighter future.

In the realm of personal growth, forgiveness acts as a cornerstone—a profound act of self-love and empowerment. It signals your commitment to your own well-being and growth, demonstrating your willingness to move beyond pain and cultivate an environment where healing and positive change can thrive. Ultimately, forgiveness is not a sign of weakness, but a testament to your inner strength and resilience, as you choose the path of liberation over the confinement of grudges.

Question #82

If you could restore one broken relationship, who would it be with?

       In the journey of personal growth, this question invites you to explore the intricate tapestry of your connections and the profound impact they have on your life. It prompts you to reflect on those relationships that have weathered storms, where fractures have formed, yet where the potential for healing and reconciliation still lingers. This question isn't just about revisiting the past; it's about acknowledging the power of human connection to shape your present and future.

       In contemplating this question, you may find yourself revisiting moments of vulnerability, misunderstanding, and perhaps even regret. It's also a gateway to introspection, growth, and the possibility of transformation. Restoring a broken relationship isn't solely about nostalgia or seeking closure; it's an act of courage that requires empathy, humility, and a willingness to acknowledge our own role in the fracture.

Deciding which relationship to restore calls for a deep understanding of your values and priorities. It's about recognizing the individuals who have played pivotal roles in your journey, those whose presence have left an indelible mark on your growth. Restoration isn't about erasing the past, but about reimagining the future—a future where connection, understanding, and growth are prioritized over resentment or distance.

While the prospect of restoring a broken relationship might be daunting, it also holds the potential for profound rewards. It's an opportunity to embark on a path of healing, open communication, and renewed connection. It's a testament to your capacity for growth and forgiveness, a testament to our ability to evolve and transform not just as individuals, but as part of a larger network of human relationships.

Ultimately, the question invites you to confront the complexities of human nature, the beauty of vulnerability, and the hope that even in the face of rupture, there exists the possibility for reconciliation. It's an invitation to extend a hand, to rebuild bridges, and to rewrite the narrative of a relationship from one of brokenness to one of resilience and renewal. In this exploration, you discover the capacity of personal growth not just to enrich your life, but to mend the bonds that connect you to others in meaningful and transformative ways.

Question #83

How does your childhood continue to influence you on your journey of personal growth?

      This question delves into the profound layers of our past, recognizing that the imprints left by our early experiences shape the contours of our present selves and the path we tread toward personal evolution. It prompts us to acknowledge the intricate tapestry woven by our upbringing—both the moments of joy and the challenges we faced—as they ripple through the currents of our adulthood.

      In embracing this question, we unlock a gateway to self-discovery, recognizing that our formative years have a lasting impact on our beliefs, behaviors, and perspectives. The question invites us to explore the roots of our strengths and vulnerabilities, to understand the patterns that have shaped our responses to the world, and to navigate the terrain of personal growth with a newfound awareness.

      This reflection isn't about dwelling on the past, but about illuminating the hidden threads that connect our childhood experiences to our present circumstances. It's a voyage that requires introspection and compassion—a journey to embrace our younger selves with empathy, acknowledge the lessons we've learned, and untangle the threads that might still hold us back.

By confronting the echoes of our past, we empower ourselves to cultivate intentional change. We gain insight into how certain narratives or beliefs were woven into the fabric of our identity, and we're better equipped to rewrite those narratives, should they no longer serve our growth. This question encourages us to unravel the complexities of our inner world, to understand the origins of our motivations, and to channel these insights into our pursuit of transformation.

As we recognize the ongoing influence of our childhood, we tap into a wellspring of resilience. We can draw upon the wisdom that stems from both our triumphs and tribulations, using it as a foundation for our aspirations. The journey of personal growth is a tapestry of interconnected threads, and our childhood experiences form a vital part of that intricate design. In embracing this connection, we cultivate a deeper sense of self-understanding, authenticity, and empowerment as we move forward on the path of self-discovery and transformation.

Question #84

What is your greatest accomplishment?

When reflecting on your journey and personal achievements, it could be challenging to single out one particular accomplishment as the greatest. Each milestone is significant and uniquely contributes to your growth and development.

This question serves as a mirror to our journey of personal growth, inviting us to reflect on the milestones that have defined our sense of achievement and self-worth. It urges us to recognize that accomplishment isn't solely measured by external recognition or grand gestures, but also by the internal transformations we've undergone. This question encourages us to sift through the tapestry of our experiences and pinpoint the moments that have left an indelible mark on our path.

In exploring our greatest accomplishment, we delve into the essence of our aspirations and values. It prompts us to consider not only the destination but the journey itself—the challenges we've overcome, the lessons we've learned, and the growth we've experienced. This reflection underscores that personal growth is a continuous endeavor, woven into the fabric of every achievement, big or small.

While this question nudges us to celebrate our successes, it also encourages humility and a sense of gratitude. Acknowledging our greatest accomplishment doesn't imply that our journey has concluded; rather, it illuminates the stepping-stones that have brought us this far. It's an opportunity to reevaluate our goals, to realign our aspirations with our evolving self, and to redefine what accomplishment means to us as we traverse the evolving landscape of personal growth.

Furthermore, this question reminds us that our journey is unique, and our greatest accomplishments are as diverse as our individual stories. Each person's path to growth is distinct, and what we deem as our greatest accomplishment may differ widely from another's. By recognizing and sharing our personal triumphs, we contribute to a collective narrative of resilience, perseverance, and the pursuit of becoming our best selves.

In essence, the question beckons us to take stock of our journey, honoring the distances we've traveled and the growth we've embraced along the way. It encourages us to view accomplishment as a continuum rather than a static destination, reminding us that the pursuit of personal growth is a lifelong adventure—a journey enriched by the milestones that highlight our resilience, purpose, and transformation.

While the concept of the "greatest" accomplishment is subjective and personal, the journey of striving towards and achieving goals truly matters. Each milestone, no matter how big or small, contributes to our narrative and shapes who we become. Recognizing and celebrating our accomplishments, big and small, helps foster a sense of self-worth, confidence, and the motivation to keep pushing forward in pursuit of new heights.

Question #85

Who do you go to for advice?

When seeking guidance and advice, I hope you are fortunate enough to have a diverse network of individuals you can turn to for support. The people you rely on for advice vary depending on the nature of the situation and the expertise required.

This question draws us into the intricate web of relationships that shape our personal growth journey. It prompts us to reflect on the sources of guidance and wisdom we seek as we navigate life's complexities. This question acknowledges that growth is not a solitary endeavor; it thrives within the tapestry of connections we've cultivated.

Exploring our choice of advisors offers insight into our values, aspirations, and the kind of support we need. The individuals we turn to hold a mirror to our trust, respect, and the lessons we've gleaned from their experiences. Whether they are mentors, friends, family members, or experts in various fields, our advisors provide us with perspectives that enrich our personal development.

This question invites us to acknowledge that seeking advice isn't a sign of weakness but rather a testament to our humility and openness to learning. By embracing the wisdom of others, we acknowledge the vast pool of knowledge that exists beyond our own perspectives. It is through these exchanges that we broaden our understanding, refine our decisions, and refine our path to growth.

In discerning who we approach for advice, we also navigate the delicate balance between external insights and our inner intuition. While external guidance is valuable, it's crucial to align it with our own values and goals, using it to refine our understanding rather than dictate our choices. This interplay between external wisdom and inner knowing forms a critical part of our journey towards holistic personal growth.

Ultimately, the question serves as a reminder that personal growth is a collaborative endeavor. Our advisors, mentors, and confidantes weave into our narrative, providing a scaffold of support as we venture into the uncharted territories of growth. Their insights help us view challenges from different angles, discover hidden potentials, and navigate the complexities of transformation. Thus, in answering this question, we acknowledge the invaluable role these relationships play in nurturing our personal evolution.

Finding individuals with experience, empathy, and genuine care for your well-being is the key to seeking advice. Whether it's family members, trusted friends, or mentors, having a support system of people you can turn to for advice is a valuable asset that provides different perspectives and helps you make informed decisions.

Question #86

Are you independent or dependent?

You will realize that the separation between independence and dependence is not black and white. It is a spectrum on which individuals can find themselves at different points in different areas of their lives. Nurturing a healthy balance between independence and interdependence is essential for personal well-being and growth.

This question explores the delicate dance between self-sufficiency and interconnectedness on our journey of personal growth. It prompts us to examine the dynamics that shape our relationships with ourselves and others, shedding light on how we navigate autonomy and interdependence in our pursuit of becoming our best selves.

This question acknowledges that personal growth is not a solitary endeavor; it's a weaving together of our individual growth with the contributions of the world around us. It invites us to recognize that independence isn't a complete detachment from others but rather a foundation from which we build authentic connections. Likewise, dependence isn't necessarily a relinquishment of personal agency, but a recognition of the strength that stems from leaning on others when needed.

Exploring the spectrum between independence and dependence offers insight into our strengths and vulnerabilities. It urges us to question whether our quest for autonomy stems from a genuine desire for self-discovery or from a fear of vulnerability. Similarly, it prompts us to evaluate whether our willingness to lean on others is a sign of trust or a reluctance to step into our own power.

As we delve into this question, we uncover the complexity of balance. Striving for independence should not translate into isolation, and seeking support should not equate to surrendering our agency. The art lies in recognizing when to stand strong on our own and when to reach out for a helping hand. It's about fostering relationships that empower growth without stifling it, and cultivating self-reliance without shutting the door to collaboration.

Ultimately, this question encourages us to cultivate a healthy interplay between independence and dependence. By embracing our individuality while remaining open to the wisdom and contributions of others, we navigate personal growth with a harmonious blend of self-discovery, self-care, and meaningful connections. In finding this equilibrium, we pave the way for a transformative journey that respects both our autonomy and our interconnectedness.

Finding a healthy balance between independence and interdependence is a dynamic process that requires self-awareness and adaptability. It is about recognizing when to embrace autonomy and when to seek support and collaboration. Understanding and honoring both aspects allow you to navigate life with self-reliance while fostering meaningful connections and building a solid support system.

Question #87

What kind of person would you be in a world without judgment?

You may imagine yourself embodying empathy, compassion, and acceptance in a world without judgment. Without judgment, you would be free to embrace and appreciate individuals' diversity and unique experiences. You would strive to understand others deeply, actively listening to their perspectives and seeking common ground instead of hastily forming opinions.

In such a world, you would be more open-minded and less prone to making assumptions or stereotyping. Instead, you would approach interactions with genuine curiosity, eager to learn from others and celebrate their differences. Without judgment, you would prioritize connection over comparison, fostering a sense of unity and shared humanity.

This question invites us to explore the depths of our authenticity and self-expression on the canvas of a judgment-free world. It prompts us to envision a reality where the weight of external evaluation is lifted, allowing us to thrive without the constraints of societal expectations and opinions. This question is an invitation to peel away the layers of self-censorship and uncover the essence of our true selves.

In contemplating this question, we unearth the profound impact that judgment has on our thoughts, actions, and identity. It urges us to consider how our decisions might change, the risks we would take, and the passions we would wholeheartedly pursue if the shadows of judgment were erased. This exploration resonates with the longing for liberation from the fear of scrutiny, enabling us to embrace our authentic desires and aspirations.

Reflecting on a world without judgment also encourages us to empathize with others. Just as we would experience the freedom to express ourselves, so too would those around us. It compels us to recognize the diversity of perspectives and choices that flourish when the shackles of judgment are removed, fostering an atmosphere of compassion, acceptance, and mutual growth.

In envisioning this judgment-free world, we tap into a wellspring of self-discovery and personal growth. We encounter aspects of ourselves that might have been buried beneath layers of conformity and self-consciousness. This question is a call to reflect on the values that guide our actions, the passions that light our path, and the unfiltered version of ourselves that emerges when the fear of judgment is removed.

While the reality of a completely judgment-free world might be a distant dream, this question has the power to transform our perspective on the present. It empowers us to actively shed the weight of external opinions, to embrace our individuality, and to cultivate environments that foster authenticity and growth. By nurturing self-acceptance and understanding, we create pockets of this liberated world within our own lives—a space where personal growth flourishes in the absence of judgment's shadow.

Question #88

Are you judgmental toward others?

Reflecting on your behavior and mindset, you might recognize that there may have been times when you were judgmental toward others. We judge based on our perspectives, biases, and preconceived notions. However, you may have realized the importance of challenging and addressing this judgmental mindset.

Being judgmental often stems from a lack of understanding or empathy towards others. It can lead to unfair assessments and a narrow-minded view of individuals and their experiences. We must learn that proper growth and personal development come from adopting a more open and compassionate approach.

To overcome judgmental tendencies, you must practice empathy and seek to understand different perspectives. This involves setting aside your assumptions and taking the time to listen and learn from others. By encouraging empathy, you recognize that everyone has unique journeys and circumstances that shape their actions and choices.

Self-awareness is vital in combating judgmental behavior. We must regularly reflect on our thoughts and attitudes, questioning the underlying biases that may influence our judgments. This self-reflection could help you identify and challenge your assumptions, allowing for more open-mindedness and understanding.

Your goal should be to create a non-judgmental and inclusive environment where individuals feel respected and valued for who they are. By fostering empathy, embracing diversity, and promoting understanding, you can strive to foster a less judgmental mindset and be more accepting of others.

Question #89

Do you find yourself striving for perfection? How might the pursuit of perfection be causing difficulties in your life, and what steps can you take to release its grip?

This may or may not resonate with you. Thinking back on tendencies and behaviors, you may acknowledge that you have struggled with perfectionism at various times. The constant pursuit of perfection could have caused external and internal pressures, leading to stress, anxiety, and a fear of failure. You may have come to understand that perfectionism is a double-edged sword, as it may drive you to achieve high standards but also leaves you feeling perpetually dissatisfied.

Perfectionism can obstruct progress and growth by creating unrealistic expectations and an unhealthy fixation on outcomes. It often leads to self-criticism and a fear of making mistakes, stifling creativity, and limiting one's willingness to take risks. It can also strain relationships, as you may project your expectations onto others and struggle to accept their imperfections.

To let go of perfectionism, you are learning to embrace the concept of "good enough." Attempt to shift your focus from ideal outcomes to the process and the journey itself. This involves setting realistic goals and acknowledging that mistakes and setbacks are inherent to learning and growth. Remind yourself that progress and effort are more important than absolute perfection.

Practicing self-compassion is crucial in releasing the grip of perfectionism and learning to treat yourself with kindness and understanding, celebrating your achievements, and accepting your flaws. By encouraging self-compassion, you can break free from the cycle of perfectionism and allow yourself to learn, grow, and experience joy in pursuing your goals.

Letting go of perfectionism requires a shift in mindset and a commitment to self-acceptance. It is a process that involves embracing imperfections, challenging self-imposed standards, and prioritizing overall well-being and happiness over unattainable ideals. By practicing self-compassion, embracing mistakes as learning opportunities, and focusing on progress rather than perfection, you can free yourself from the pain and limitations that perfectionism imposes.

In the quest for excellence, it's common to embrace the role of a perfectionist. However, this pursuit can inadvertently give rise to challenges, potentially causing undue stress, stifling creativity, and fostering self-doubt. By acknowledging the impact of perfectionism and cultivating a mindset of self-compassion and flexibility, we can pave the way for greater personal growth, innovation, and overall well-being.

Question #90

What type of characteristics do you look for in your ideal life-partner?

Several qualities come to mind when considering the characteristics you seek in an ideal partner. First, consider compatibility and shared values. Next, you must connect with someone who aligns with your core beliefs, goals, and aspirations. Finally, mutual respect, trust, and effective communication are fundamental to building a solid foundation for a healthy and fulfilling relationship.

Also, one should appreciate kindness and empathy in a partner. A compassionate and understanding nature fosters an environment of support and emotional connection. Therefore, look for someone empathetic, considerate, and supportive, as these qualities contribute to a harmonious and nurturing partnership.

You may also value intelligence and a sense of humor. Intellectual stimulation and the ability to engage in meaningful conversations may be necessary. A partner with a curious mind who shares knowledge and embraces a lighthearted approach to life can enhance the depth and enjoyment of the relationship.

Within the landscape of personal growth, the criteria we seek in an ideal life partner extend far beyond surface compatibility. Delving into this question involves envisioning a partner who not only shares our goals and visions but also encourages us to reach for new heights. In this exploration, we unearth the significance of emotional intimacy, effective communication, and a shared sense of purpose. By prioritizing a partner who aligns with our aspirations and values, we forge a profound connection that propels us toward individual and mutual growth, fostering a relationship that becomes a dynamic catalyst for our collective journey of self-discovery and transformation.

Within the intricate realm of personal growth, the concept of attraction transcends mere surface appeal. It encompasses a magnetic force that draws us towards individuals whose qualities resonate deeply with our evolving sense of self. Attraction isn't confined to physical attributes; it's a dance between energies, a harmony of values, dreams, and aspirations that intertwine seamlessly. As we grow, our perception of attraction evolves—it becomes a reflection of our inner transformation, pulling us toward those who mirror the qualities we aspire to embody. This deeper level of attraction ignites connections that fuel our journey of self-discovery, mutual understanding, and shared progress. By recognizing the multi-dimensional nature of attraction, we elevate our relationships to be not just sources of comfort, but profound catalysts for our ongoing personal evolution.

May you seek someone who values personal growth and is committed to self-improvement. A partner who is open to learning, willing to face challenges, and dedicated to personal development can inspire you and foster growth within the relationship. While everyone's ideal partner may differ, these qualities resonate with most as essential components of a fulfilling and harmonious relationship. We can create a strong bond based on mutual understanding, support, and growth by seeking a partner who embodies these characteristics.

Question #91

What aspect of the world do you aspire to transform? How can you initiate the process of cultivating this transformation within your own life?

This question prompts individuals to reflect on the issues that resonate deeply with them, urging them to step beyond their personal sphere and consider the broader world. This reflection is the seed from which the desire for transformation sprouts.

The question goes beyond a mere acknowledgment of global challenges; it prompts action on a personal level. By considering how one can initiate the process of cultivating change within their own life, individuals embark on a path of empowerment. This often involves aligning personal values with intentional actions, encouraging the ripple effect that transformation often brings. Whether it's by adopting new habits, refining perspectives, or engaging in meaningful conversations, the process of personal transformation becomes intertwined with the greater aspiration to impact the world positively.

Ultimately, the question ignites a process of synthesis, where one's inner aspirations blend with their role in the larger narrative of humanity. It underscores the undeniable interconnectivity between personal growth and global change, reminding us that every individual has the potential to be a catalyst for transformation, both within themselves and the world around them.

One aspect that you may be passionate about in transforming is mental health awareness and destigmatization. The prevalence of mental health issues is a global concern, and you may be dedicated to fostering a more compassionate and understanding society. To cultivate this transformation within your own life, you can prioritize self-care and mental well-being. This includes regular mindfulness practices, open conversations about mental health with friends and family, and advocating for mental health resources in their community. By openly sharing your journey and encouraging conversations, you can aim to create a safe space for others to seek support and feel empowered to address your own mental health challenges.

Another aspect of the world you may want to contribute to is the transformation of education systems. The traditional model often falls short in preparing students for the complexities of the modern world. To instigate change, you may explore ways to enhance your own learning journey. You may actively seek out diverse sources of knowledge, engaging in online courses, and cultivating critical thinking and problem-solving skills. By becoming lifelong learners and sharing your experiences with unconventional learning paths, you may hope to inspire a shift towards more dynamic and adaptable educational approaches that foster creativity, curiosity, and practical skills among students.

By initiating changes within your own life and openly sharing your journey, you may aspire to contribute to larger-scale shifts in these areas, creating a more sustainable, compassionate, and forward-thinking global community.

Question #92

Do you feel free? What is keeping you from being/feeling free?

Whether you feel free prompts deep introspection into the constraints and limitations that may impede your sense of freedom; while freedom is a subjective experience, recognize that certain factors can restrict or shape this feeling in your life. One significant aspect that can hinder freedom is fear. Fear of judgment, failure, or uncertainty can hold you back from fully embracing your desires and pursuing what truly sets your soul on fire. Overcoming these fears requires courage and a willingness to step outside your comfort zone, allowing yourself to take risks and explore uncharted territories.

Another factor that can limit your sense of freedom is self-imposed expectations and societal norms. The pressure to conform to societal standards, meet certain milestones, or live up to others' expectations can create a sense of constraint and interrupt your authentic expression. Embracing your individuality and embracing the path that resonates with your true self can help you break free from these constraints and develop a sense of liberation.

External circumstances such as financial obligations, responsibilities, and obligations can also influence your perceived freedom. Therefore, assessing whether these obligations align with your values and priorities is crucial. By balancing meeting responsibilities and carving out time for personal fulfillment, you can navigate towards a greater sense of freedom.

Achieving a sense of freedom requires introspection, self-awareness, and a willingness to confront and challenge the barriers that hold you back. It is an ongoing journey of self-discovery and consciously making choices that align with your authentic desires. By actively working towards shedding limiting beliefs, embracing vulnerability, and cultivating a mindset of possibility, you can move closer to true freedom.

Question #93

Are you hiding a part of yourself from the world? If so, in what way?

Whether you are hiding a part of yourself from the world evokes a profound reflection on the aspects of your identity or experiences that you may keep hidden. In truth, sometimes you conceal certain parts of your authentic self, often out of fear of judgment or rejection. One way in which you may hide is by suppressing your genuine emotions and vulnerabilities. For example, you may put up a facade of strength and stoicism, fearing that showing your exposure will be perceived as a weakness. However, by doing so, you deny yourself the opportunity for genuine connections and authentic relationships.

Another way in which you may be hiding is by conforming to societal expectations and norms. To fit in or be accepted, you may downplay certain aspects of your personality or interests that do not align with the prevailing standards. However, by doing this, you sacrifice your authentic essence and compromise your individuality. Embracing your uniqueness and expressing your true self without fear of judgment is essential for living a fulfilled and authentic life.

You may hide parts of your past or personal experiences that you perceive as shameful or embarrassing. These hidden parts may stem from mistakes you have made or past failures that you wish to forget. However, concealing these aspects denies you the opportunity for growth, healing, and learning. Therefore, embracing our past, acknowledging our imperfections, and using them as stepping-stones for personal development and resilience is essential.

Acknowledging the parts of yourself that you hide is the first step towards self-acceptance and living authentically. It requires vulnerability, courage, and a willingness to embrace your true self. By gradually unveiling and embracing these hidden aspects, you can improve and create a deeper connection with yourself and others, fostering a sense of belonging and fulfillment.

Question #94

Are you prone to jealousy? If so, how can you change this part of yourself?

This question invites a thoughtful examination of your tendencies and reactions concerning jealousy. It is true that, at times, you may find yourself experiencing feelings of envy or insecurity, particularly when comparing yourself to others or perceiving their successes as a threat to your self-worth. However, jealousy can be complex and challenging, often resulting from feelings of inadequacy or fear of missing out.

To change this part of yourself, you must first recognize that jealousy is not a productive or healthy mindset. On the contrary, it can delay personal growth, strain relationships, and create unnecessary negativity. You can start by developing self-awareness and introspection to understand the root causes of your jealousy. Then, by identifying triggers and examining the underlying beliefs and insecurities fueling these feelings, you can begin to challenge and reframe your perspectives.

Practicing gratitude is another powerful tool in shifting away from jealousy. Cultivating gratitude allows you to focus on the abundance in your life and appreciate your unique path rather than comparing yourself to others. It helps to shift your mindset from scarcity to abundance and fosters a sense of contentment.

Fostering a mindset of collaboration and support rather than competition can be transformative. Celebrating the successes of others and genuinely wishing them well can create a positive and supportive environment. By nurturing genuine connections and embracing a mindset of abundance and collaboration, you can gradually diminish the hold that jealousy has over you, fostering personal growth and cultivating more positive and fulfilling relationships.

Question #95

When was the last time you cried? Do you cry too often or not often enough?

The question of when you last cried invites you to reflect on your emotional vulnerability and the frequency with which you express your emotions through tears. Crying is a natural and healthy way for the body and mind to release built-up emotions and provide a liberating outlet. However, the frequency of crying can vary significantly from person to person, and there is no right or wrong amount.

The last time you cried could be a few weeks ago when you watched a heartfelt movie that resonated deeply with you. Crying is a valuable and necessary emotional release, allowing you to process and navigate complex feelings. Whether you cry too often or not often enough is subjective and varies based on individual circumstances and emotional needs.

It is essential to honor and embrace our emotions without judgment. Suppressing tears can be detrimental, leading to emotional repression and potentially negatively impacting mental and physical well-being. On the other hand, crying excessively may indicate unresolved emotional issues that require attention and support.

The key is cultivating emotional self-awareness and developing a healthy relationship with our emotions. By allowing ourselves to cry when needed, we can acknowledge and validate our feelings, promoting emotional well-being and fostering a deeper understanding of ourselves. Finding a balance that feels authentic to our individual experiences and needs is essential.

Question #96

In what ways could you be simplifying your life?

The question of simplifying your life prompts you to examine the various areas where you can reduce complexity and create a more streamlined and balanced lifestyle. Simplifying your life is about eliminating unnecessary clutter, commitments, and distractions that can drain your energy and hinder your overall well-being.

One way you could simplify your life is by decluttering your physical space. This involves letting go of possessions that no longer serve a purpose or bring you joy. In addition, creating an organized and minimalist environment can cultivate a sense of calm and clarity. Simplifying your schedule is another important aspect. It means evaluating your commitments and priorities and learning to say no to activities or obligations that do not align with your values or contribute to your overall well-being.

Additionally, simplifying your digital life is crucial in today's fast-paced and technology-driven world. This entails minimizing screen time, decluttering digital files, and unsubscribing from unnecessary online subscriptions or notifications. By creating boundaries and being mindful of your digital consumption, you can regain focus and create space for more meaningful activities and connections.

Amidst the journey of personal growth, it's essential to consider the ways we can simplify our lives by shedding people, social obligations, or possessions that no longer align with our authentic path. By discerning and letting go of relationships that drain our energy, commitments that lack purpose, and possessions that clutter our physical and emotional space, we create room for what truly nourishes our well-being and aspirations. This intentional simplification liberates us from unnecessary burdens, allowing us to channel our focus and energy towards the people, experiences, and endeavors that resonate with our journey of self-discovery, and ultimately fostering a greater sense of clarity, meaning, and progress.

Simplifying your life is an ongoing journey that requires self-reflection and conscious choices. It is about prioritizing what truly matters, nurturing your well-being, and finding balance amidst the demands and complexities of modern life. Embracing simplicity can create more space for joy, peace, and fulfillment.

Question #97

What makes you feel truly alive?

      This question propels us to the core of our existence, urging us to explore the activities, experiences, and moments that ignite a vibrant sense of purpose and vitality within us. By identifying the sources of inspiration that evoke genuine enthusiasm, connection, and joy, we uncover the threads that weave our unique path to self-discovery. Recognizing what makes us feel truly alive guides us toward aligning our pursuits with our innermost passions, fostering a profound authenticity that fuels our personal evolution and enriches our journey towards a more vibrant and fulfilling life. In these moments, you feel a profound connection to yourself, others, and the world around you.

      One of the things that may make you feel truly alive is engaging in creative pursuits. Whether writing, painting, or playing a musical instrument, self-expression allows you to tap into your authentic voice and channel your emotions and thoughts into something tangible. Creating can bring you a sense of fulfillment and invigorates your spirit.

Another source is being in nature and spending time outdoors, whether hiking in the mountains or simply sitting by the ocean, since it could reconnect you with the beauty and wonder of the natural world. Nature's sights, sounds, and sensations awaken your senses and ground you in the present moment, filling you with a deep understanding of awe and gratitude.

Engaging in meaningful connections and shared experiences with loved ones brings you a profound sense of aliveness. Whether engaging in deep conversations, laughing together, or supporting one another through challenging times, these connections remind you of the power of human connection and the richness of being present with others.

Embracing a life that aligns with your passions, values, and authenticity makes you feel truly alive. In pursuing what brings you joy, connecting with nature, and fostering meaningful relationships, you find the energy and enthusiasm that make you feel fully alive.

Question #98

Do you display emotional intelligence?

Emotional intelligence, a cornerstone of personal growth, encompasses the ability to navigate and understand our own emotions while empathetically connecting with the emotions of others. It involves perceiving, managing, and harnessing emotions to guide our thoughts and actions, fostering improved communication, self-awareness, and interpersonal relationships. By cultivating emotional intelligence, we empower ourselves to respond thoughtfully to challenges, build deeper connections, and navigate our journey of growth with a heightened sense of empathy, resilience, and emotional well-being.

Whether you display emotional intelligence prompts you to reflect on your ability to recognize, understand, and manage your own emotions, as well as navigate and empathize with the feelings of others. Having emotional intelligence is a crucial asset that enables you to develop healthy relationships, make sound decisions, and effectively communicate your needs and feelings.

In examining your emotional intelligence, strive to be self-aware and attuned to your emotions. This involves recognizing and acknowledging your feelings, understanding their underlying causes, and being mindful of how they influence your thoughts and behaviors. By cultivating self-awareness, you are better equipped to respond to situations thoughtfully and intentionally rather than reacting impulsively based on fleeting emotions.

Emotional intelligence entails empathizing with others and understanding their perspectives and feelings. Strive to listen actively and attentively, seeking to understand not only the words someone is saying but also the emotions they are conveying. This empathetic understanding helps you foster more meaningful connections and respond with compassion and sensitivity to the needs and experiences of others.

Emotional intelligence involves the ability to regulate and manage emotions effectively. This means developing healthy coping mechanisms, practicing self-care, and finding constructive ways to express and process emotions. By cultivating emotional resilience, you can navigate challenges and conflicts with tremendous poise and find healthier outlets for emotional expression.

Emotional intelligence is an ongoing journey of self-reflection and growth. You can enhance your relationships, decision-making, and overall well-being by continually honing your self-awareness, empathy, and emotional management skills.

Question #99

How do you define success?

      The concept of success is deeply personal and varies from individual to individual. Success is not solely defined by external achievements or material possessions but, rather, by the fulfillment and contentment you experience in various aspects of your life. It encompasses a sense of purpose, growth, and aligning your actions with your values and aspirations.

      True success lies in the pursuit of meaningful goals and the continuous improvement of oneself. It is about setting and working towards personal milestones that align with your passions, talents, and values. It involves embracing challenges, learning from failures, and persevering with determination and resilience.

      Success extends beyond individual accomplishments, fostering positive relationships and positively impacting others. It involves being a source of inspiration, support, and encouragement for those around you and contributing to the well-being and happiness of others. Success is not a solitary endeavor but a collective journey of growth and shared achievements.

Success is a dynamic and ever-evolving concept shaped by your aspirations, values, and the mark you want to leave on the world. It is not a destination to be reached but a continuous process of self-discovery, growth, and making a meaningful difference in your own life and the lives of others.

Success encompasses the fulfillment of both personal goals and a sense of contentment. It involves manifesting aspirations through focused intentions and aligning actions with positive thoughts. The law of attraction reinforces this idea by emphasizing the power of maintaining a constructive mindset to draw in opportunities and circumstances that resonate with one's goals. This involves consistent and inspired action, resilience in the face of challenges, and the transformation of self-limiting beliefs into empowering ones.

Through practicing gratitude and mindfulness, one can maintain momentum and recognize the progress made, thereby creating a dynamic interplay between manifestation, the law of attraction, and the journey toward success.

In essence, success intertwines with the principles of manifestation and the law of attraction by underscoring the significance of intention-driven actions and a positive mindset. It's about envisioning objectives with clarity and allowing that vision to guide one's efforts. As one navigates obstacles and remains persistent, the law of attraction reinforces the notion that the energy expended through thoughts and actions shapes the reality experienced. By embracing these concepts, success becomes not only a destination but a holistic and continuous journey of growth and self-discovery.

In the realm of personal growth, defining success extends beyond external achievements to encompass a sense of fulfillment derived from aligning our actions with our core values and aspirations. Success is marked by an ongoing journey of self-discovery, continuous learning, and the pursuit of meaningful goals that resonate with our authentic selves. It involves cultivating inner contentment, nurturing positive relationships, and embracing personal growth as a dynamic process that empowers us to become our best selves, contributing positively to both our own well-being and the betterment of the world around us.

Question #100

What am I going to do differently now after reading this guide?

After reading "*100 Questions to Unleash Your Inner Potential: A Guide to Personal Growth and Transformation,*" I hope you are inspired to take action and make positive changes in your life. The thought-provoking questions have hopefully provided valuable insights and self-awareness, highlighting areas where you can improve and grow. Armed with this newfound knowledge, may you be determined to translate it into action.

May you be committed to prioritizing your personal growth and well-being. I hope you realize the importance of self-reflection, setting goals, and taking consistent steps toward self-improvement. Carve out dedicated time for self-reflection, journaling, and engaging in activities that nurture your mind, body, and soul.

May this motivate you to cultivate healthier habits and release any negative patterns holding you back. Whether taking better care of your physical health, developing a more positive mindset, or practicing self-compassion, commit to making intentional choices that align with your values and contribute to your overall well-being.

Recognize the significance of surrounding yourself with positive and supportive individuals who bring out the best in you. Seek meaningful connections and foster relationships with people who inspire, challenge, and uplift you. Additionally, actively contribute to the well-being of others and strive to make a positive impact in their lives.

This book has hopefully inspired a sense of empowerment and motivation within you. Be determined to take charge of your life, embrace personal growth, and live purposefully and authentically. By translating these reflections into tangible actions, you can create a more fulfilling and meaningful life for yourself and those around you.

Embracing Personal Growth and Unleashing Your Inner Potential

"100 Questions to Unleash Your Inner Potential: A Guide to Personal Growth and Transformation" invites you to a transformative journey of self-discovery and empowerment. Throughout this book, we have explored many thought-provoking questions designed to unlock your hidden potential and ignite a passion for personal growth.

Remember, the power lies within you. Each question has served as a key to unlocking a new level of self-awareness, inspiring you to dive deeper into your dreams, fears, strengths, weaknesses, and aspirations. You have completed a journey of self-discovery and personal transformation by engaging with these questions honestly and introspectively.

As you continue your journey beyond these pages, please reflect on the insights you have gained and take proactive steps toward positive change. Embrace the growth opportunities, confront your limiting beliefs, and set bold goals aligning with your desires. Finally, embrace self-compassion, knowing that growth takes time and setbacks are part of the journey.

Remember that personal growth is not a destination but a lifelong process. As you continue to explore these questions and embark on your unique path, may you find the courage, resilience, and determination to unleash your inner potential and create a life that genuinely reflects your authentic self.

Believe in yourself, embrace the journey, the challenges, and the limitless possibilities. Your potential is boundless, and the world is waiting for the brilliance that lies within you.

Printed in Great Britain
by Amazon